One Minute Bible

FOR STARTERS

for

THE FIRST

new

9 0 - D A Y S

christians

One Minute Bible

FOR STARTERS

for
THE FIRST
new
90-DAYS
christians

LAWRENCE KIMBROUGH

HOLMAN
REFERENCE

Nashville, Tennessee

One Minute Bible for Starters
Copyright © 1999 Broadman & Holman Publishers
Nashville, Tennessee, 37234
All rights reserved

ISBN 0-8054-9386-7

Production Staff
Executive Editor: David Shepherd
Editor: Lawrence Kimbrough
Project Editor: Lloyd Mullens
Design Team: Wendell Overstreet, Stephen Phanco
Production: Kevin Kunce

Library of Congress Cataloging-in-Publication Data
Kimbrough, Lawrence, 1963–
        Kimbrough, Lawrence, editor [i.e. author].
        p.   cm.
        Includes bibliographical references.
        ISBN 0-8054-9386-7
        1. Devotional calendars. 2. Christian life quaotations,
        maxims, etc. I. Title
BV4811.K455 1999
242'.5—dc21   99–15734
                                                   CIP

Printed in the United States
1 2 3 4 5 6 03 02 01 00 99
                D

One Minute Bible

To: _____ Greg _____

From: _____ James _____

_____ Christmas 99 _____
cause I know I need all of the Help
I can get.

Your accountability partner: _____

Phone number: _____

"I thank my God every time I remember you . . . being confident of this, that he who began a good work in you will carry it on to completion until the day of Christ Jesus."

Philippians 1:3, 6

Hi.
Come on in.

B oil it all down, and the outlook for your life basically hinges on one single decision—whether to trust your future into the hands of Jesus Christ or to take your chances. The rest, as they say, is just details.

Congratulations on making the right choice.

The next good choice you need to make, though, is to not let it stop there. The *One Minute Bible for Starters* is the place to begin letting this life-size decision make a real difference in your daily life. The chapters are short, but the truths are deep. And you can find yourself growing in Christ in a hurry.

Each short, 2-page chapter (you can easily read one a day) includes a Bible passage that'll only take about a minute to read, followed by a little explanation. It's that simple. You'll also find room to jot some notes to yourself, as well as a highlighted Bible verse that gives you a quick truth to hold onto.

Another good choice is to find a dedicated Christian friend—a family member, a co-worker, someone from your church—who would commit to reading through the book with you, so that when you get together you can ask your questions and learn even more.

But however you decide to use it, we hope this book will help you know God better and understand how much He loves you.

He has some wonderful things in store for your life. Here are some of them…*For Starters*.

Table of Contents

Section One
Time To Make A Change

Section Two
Building On The Basics

Section Three
Sizing Up The Enemy

Section Four
A New Way Of Thinking

Section Five
Sure Signs Of Growth

Section Six
Nice Things To Know

Section Seven
Stepping Out On Faith

Section Eight
Second Line Of Defense

Section Nine
From Here To Eternity

SECTION 1

Time to Make a Change

Whether you're just now coming to Christ, or just getting serious about it for the first time in a long time, you'll find that God is always willing to join you on the starting line, but never content with letting you remain the way you are. Or the way you've been. Want to see some changes in your life? You've come to the right place.

Why Me?
Why Now?

How God Draws You to Himself

You may have felt like you were the one doing all the chasing. But God's been after you a long time.

Then Jesus declared, "I am the bread of life. He who comes to me will never go hungry, and he who believes in me will never be thirsty. . . .

"All that the Father gives me will come to me, and whoever comes to me I will never drive away. For I have come down from heaven not to do my will but to do the will of him who sent me. And this is the will of him who sent me, that I shall lose none of all that he has given me, but raise them up at the last day. For my Father's will is that everyone who looks to the Son and believes in him shall have eternal life, and I will raise him up at the last day. . . ."

"No one can come to me unless the Father who sent me draws him, and I will raise him up at the last day. . . ."

For Jesus had known from the beginning which of them did not believe and who would betray him. He went on to say, "This is why I told you that no one can come to me unless the Father has enabled him. . . ."

"I have loved you with an everlasting love; I have drawn you with loving-kindness."

Scripture

John 6:35, 37-40, 44, 64b-65;
Jeremiah 31:3b

DEFINING MOMENTS

Calling your conversion experience a decision for Christ doesn't begin to convey the truth of the matter. Yes, you made a decision based on your own free will. Yes, you were perfectly free to make a different choice than you did.

But look at the whole thing on balance—from God's perspective—and suddenly your decision to follow Jesus looks a lot less like a bold move on your part and a lot more like a stunning victory on His part.

He fashioned everything there is about you in His own mind. He set you in a particular time and place. He's been carefully arranging people, situations, and events in your life, waving His arms in front of your face, pleading with you to look back, to see the cross, to know the love that paid every last dime on your escalating debt of sins, to experience more freedom and joy and peace and contentment than you ever thought possible.

Looks like your hardest decision was trying to say no all this time.

> "How could the initiative lie on my side? If Shakespeare and Hamlet could ever meet, it must be Shakespeare's doing."
>
> —C. S. Lewis

NEXT UP *Before you can get too far down the road of Christian living, you must first take a good, hard look at yourself. And see how you got into this shape to begin with.*

Notes

Remember Your Roots

The Rise and Fall of Man

God created man in His own image. But it didn't take us long to think we could cut a better deal.

Now the serpent was more crafty than any of the wild animals the Lord God had made. He said to the woman, "Did God really say, 'You must not eat from any tree in the garden'?"

The woman said to the serpent, "We may eat fruit from the trees in the garden, but God did say, 'You must not eat fruit from the tree that is in the middle of the garden, and you must not touch it, or you will die.'"

"You will not surely die," the serpent said to the woman. . . .

When the woman saw that the fruit of the tree was good for food and pleasing to the eye, and also desirable for gaining wisdom, she took some and ate it. She also gave some to her husband, who was with her, and he ate it.

Then the eyes of both of them were opened, and they realized they were naked; so they sewed fig leaves together and made coverings for themselves.

Then the man and his wife heard the sound of the Lord God as he was walking in the garden in the cool of the day, *and they hid from the Lord God among the trees of the garden.*

Scripture
Genesis 3:1-4, 6-8

⤴ DEFINING MOMENTS

Say hello to the deadwood in your spiritual family tree. They go by the names Adam and Eve. And they've taken you far away from your roots. Not that we'd have done any differently had we been in their bare feet, but Adam and Eve's decline into deception cost them much more than a nice, cozy home in the garden spot of the world. It cost the entire human family everything God had created it to be.

Because of their sin—or the Fall, as it's commonly called—mankind refused his rightful, original place of perfect, guilt-free fellowship with God, and landed with a thud on a dark, remote nowhere land a million miles from home—spiritually depraved, hopelessly lost.

> "The Bible enables people to solve the dilemma facing them. They can understand both their greatness and their cruelty."
> —Francis Schaeffer

Ever since then, the human quest has been to rediscover his lost worth, to understand why his innate desire to be better than he is—and to enjoy a relationship with a God bigger than himself—has always ended in such disappointing failure. There's only one way back. And you've found it. Say hello to Jesus Christ.

NEXT UP — *Through the sacrifice of the cross, that fallen person that used to be you has now been reinstated with your heavenly Father. So why doesn't it always feel like it?*

Good Cop, Bad Cop

The New Man and the Old

This is war. You're right in the middle of it. And choosing sides is going to be an everyday battle.

I do not understand what I do. For what I want to do I do not do, but what I hate I do. And if I do what I do not want to do, I agree that the law is good. As it is, it is no longer I myself who do it, but it is sin living in me.

I know that nothing good lives in me, that is, in my sinful nature. For I have the desire to do what is good, but I cannot carry it out. For what I do is not the good I want to do; no, the evil I do not want to do—this I keep on doing.

Now if I do what I do not want to do, it is no longer I who do it, but it is sin living in me that does it.

So I find this law at work: *When I want to do good, evil is right there with me.* For in my inner being I delight in God's law; but I see another law at work in the members of my body, waging war against the law of my mind and making me a prisoner of the law of sin at work within my members.

What a wretched man I am! Who will rescue me from this body of death?

Thanks be to God—through Jesus Christ our Lord! So then, I myself in my mind am a slave to God's law, but in the sinful nature a slave to the law of sin.

Scripture
Romans 7:15-25

℃ DEFINING MOMENTS

When you welcomed Jesus into your world, He restored the blood supply to your spirit—that part of you that had been beaten and left for dead by the thugs of sin and deception. He gave you a new heart, complete with a guarantee of full protection against the punishment of hell, against the fear and finality of the grave. He placed in you His own Holy Spirit to give you a new way of thinking, a fresh awareness of God's presence, and a promise that one day your faith would pay off with a one-way ticket to paradise.

> "God will no longer be a cause of dread to me. I very soon find, however, that I am going to be a great cause of trouble to myself."
>
> —Watchman Nee

But look who's still hanging around. Your heart may be in heaven, but God's left your feet here on the ground, where the person you used to be can still have a say in your choices and remind you how much fun you all used to have together.

Don't be surprised when civil war breaks out in your heart, when you're torn between the God you love and the temptations that still know how to play your song. Your sinful self is beaten, but he's not going without a fight. Get ready, though. He has his weaknesses, too.

NEXT UP *Since old habits don't go away overnight, and may continue to be a nagging source of frustration and (at times) failure, where does the victory start coming in?*

Power in Your Corner

Your All-Sufficiency in Christ

There's no way to underestimate the struggle of Christian living. Or the power God's put in you.

I keep asking that the God of our Lord Jesus Christ, the glorious Father, may give you the Spirit of wisdom and revelation, so that you may know him better. I pray also that the eyes of your heart may be enlightened in order that you may know the hope to which he has called you, the riches of his glorious inheritance in the saints, and his incomparably great power for us who believe. . . .

I pray that out of his glorious riches he may strengthen you with power through his Spirit in your inner being, so that Christ may dwell in your hearts through faith.

And I pray that you, being rooted and established in love, may have power, together with all the saints, to grasp how wide and long and high and deep is the love of Christ, and to know this love that surpasses knowledge—*that you may be filled to the measure of all the fullness of God.*

Now to him who is able to do immeasurably more than all we ask or imagine, according to his power that is at work within us, to him be glory in the church and in Christ Jesus throughout all generations, for ever and ever! Amen.

Scripture

Ephesians 1:17-19; 3:16-21

ᘺ DEFINING MOMENTS

Trusting God to help you overcome your sins and shortcomings sounds so spiritual, doesn't it? Turning everything over to God, letting God handle your problems, giving your burdens to the Lord . . . can't argue with the wisdom there.

But when it's just you and your bad temper, or your runaway sex drive, or your weakness for cherry cheesecake, where do you find the strength to say no?

You might not guess it to look at you, but you have available to you—right now—the same kind of power that God "exerted in Christ when he raised him from the dead" (Eph. 1:20). And as you begin facing even your toughest challenges with the weapons of prayer, Bible truth, worship, thanksgiving, accountability, and other specific strategies that you'll begin gaining through experience, you'll see sin's deception for what it is, you'll turn your back on habits that have had your number for years, and your heart for instant gratification will be changed into a heart that knows where its power lies.

> "Just as He delivered us from the overall reign of sin, so He has made ample provision for us to win the daily skirmishes against sin."
>
> —Jerry Bridges

Notes

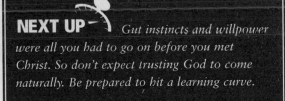

NEXT UP *Gut instincts and willpower were all you had to go on before you met Christ. So don't expect trusting God to come naturally. Be prepared to hit a learning curve.*

One Step At a Time

Learning to Walk with God

Like starting a new job or moving to a new city, learning to think like a Christian takes some time.

Therefore, rid yourselves of all malice and all deceit, hypocrisy, envy, and slander of every kind. Like newborn babies, crave pure spiritual milk, so that by it you may grow up in your salvation, now that you have tasted that the Lord is good.

As you come to him, the living Stone—rejected by men but chosen by God and precious to him—you also, like living stones, are being built into a spiritual house to be a holy priesthood, offering spiritual sacrifices acceptable to God through Jesus Christ. . . .

Anyone who lives on milk, being still an infant, is not acquainted with the teaching about righteousness. But solid food is for the mature, who by constant use have trained themselves to distinguish good from evil.

Therefore let us leave the elementary teachings about Christ and go on to maturity, not laying again the foundation of repentance from acts that lead to death, and of faith in God, instruction about baptisms, the laying on of hands, the resurrection of the dead, and eternal judgment. . . .

But grow in the grace and knowledge of our Lord and Savior Jesus Christ.

Scripture

1 Peter 2:1-5; Hebrews 5:13-6:2; 2 Peter 3:18

DEFINING MOMENTS

No one enters the Christian life as middle management. Just like there's only one way in—through belief in Jesus Christ and His death on the cross—there's only one way up. And it starts on the ground floor.

But don't worry. It's anything but boring in the minimum-wage mailroom of Christian maturity . . . for at least two reasons:

- Your enemy, Satan, knows that your fire is burning pretty bright right now. He also knows that you're vulnerable to a relapse (modern attention spans and commitment levels being what they are). He'll have plenty of temptations to keep you busy once the new wears off.

- But on the other hand, God promises you room for steady advancement if you're willing to work hard in His training program, committing yourself to His Word, to His church, to His tried-and-true philosophy of aspiring to bigger things by being faithful in the small things. New blessings and discoveries can spring up from all over when you're just starting out. You won't find this much joy in anyone else's company.

"There is no sweeter manner of living in the world than continuous communion with God. Only those who have experienced it can understand."

—Brother Lawrence

NEXT UP *Before anyone starts a new job, she needs to know who the boss is—not just who He is, but what He's like, what He's looking for, and how she can expect to be treated.*

Like a Little Child

Seeing God as Father

God goes by many names that describe His nature and character. But you can just call Him . . . Dad.

Yet to all who received him, to those who believed in his name, he gave the right to become children of God—children born not of natural descent, nor of human decision or a husband's will, but born of God. . . .

Those who are led by the Spirit of God are sons of God. . . . The Spirit himself testifies with our spirit that we are God's children. Now if we are children, then we are heirs—heirs of God and co-heirs with Christ, if indeed we share in his sufferings in order that we may also share in his glory. . . .

Which of you, if his son asks for bread, will give him a stone? Or if he asks for a fish, will give him a snake? If you, then, though you are evil, know how to give good gifts to your children, how much more will your Father in heaven give good gifts to those who ask him! . . .

Every good and perfect gift is from above, coming down from the Father of the heavenly lights, who does not change like shifting shadows. He chose to give us birth through the word of truth, that we might be a kind of firstfruits of all he created.

Scripture
John 1:12-13; Romans 8:14, 16-17; Matthew 7:9-11; James 1:17-18

⟅ DEFINING MOMENTS

When God wanted to put His love into terms we could understand, He painted Himself in the biblical imagery of a Father—not the kind who rants and raves, fussing about the way you keep your room or teaching you how to drive by pounding the dashboard every time you change lanes in traffic. Not the kind who's tied up (again) at work, or only visible from the waist down behind his morning paper, apparently unconcerned with the things that matter most to you.

Neither is He a doting grandfather, mindlessly doling out dollar bills so you can buy your fill of candy and bubble gum. This Father who asks you to walk with Him will ask more of you than anyone possibly could—your life, in fact, for the privilege of being on personal terms with the God of the universe. But in return, you'll receive a love that's so complete and unconditional, so honest and pure, so rich in mercy and long on patience, that you'll want nothing more than to please Him, to make Him proud of you, to find your reason for living in His gentle smile.

> "God will go out of His way to make His children feel His love for them and know their privilege and security as members of His family."
>
> —J. I. Packer

NEXT UP *Not only do you get to enjoy a close, personal relationship with God the Father; this new adopted family of yours includes a big brother you'd love to be like.*

What Would Jesus Do?

Thinking with the Mind of Christ

If you're serious about letting Christ change your life, you'll be asking yourself this question a lot.

Your attitude should be the same as that of Christ Jesus: Who, being in very nature God, did not consider equality with God something to be grasped, but made himself nothing, taking the very nature of a servant, being made in human likeness.

And being found in appearance as a man, he humbled himself and became obedient to death—even death on a cross!

Therefore God exalted him to the highest place and gave him the name that is above every name, that at the name of Jesus every knee should bow, in heaven and on earth and under the earth, and every tongue confess that Jesus Christ is Lord, to the glory of God the Father. . . .

Be imitators of God, therefore, as dearly loved children and live a life of love, just as Christ loved us and gave himself up for us as a fragrant offering and sacrifice to God. . . . *For you were once darkness, but now you are light in the Lord.* . . .

Do not conform any longer to the pattern of this world, but be transformed by the renewing of your mind. Then you will be able to test and approve what God's will is—his good, pleasing and perfect will.

Scripture

Philippians 2:5-11; Ephesians 5:1-2, 8; Romans 12:2

✺ DEFINING MOMENTS

Christ's death on the cross did a lot more than tear up your rap sheet and clear your name with the Judge. By accepting His death, you have also accepted His life— the seeds of a new character that He is forming inside you as you let His words become yours, as you begin adopting His nature of purity, trust, and humility, crowding out the self-centered clutter you've been accumulating all these years.

Christ has come to clean house, to bag up the stuff that needs to go in the garbage, to throw open the windows for fresh breezes of godly insight and perspective, to shine the revealing light of His Word into every corner of your life.

> "God's intention is that we be free from this world's mindset. When we think like God thinks, we are free from the bonds of Satan."
>
> —T. W. Hunt

As He starts to work within your everyday experiences, you'll not only begin doing things His way, but thinking the way He thinks, becoming sick to your stomach at the sight of your own unfaithfulness. Yet you are renewed to seek your thrills at no other place than the satisfying waters of Christian obedience and to filter your daily decisions through the lens of His unselfish love.

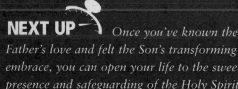

NEXT UP *Once you've known the Father's love and felt the Son's transforming embrace, you can open your life to the sweet presence and safeguarding of the Holy Spirit.*

Inside Information

Living in the Spirit

But when he, the Spirit of truth, comes, he will guide you into all truth. He will not speak on his own; he will speak only what he hears, and he will tell you what is yet to come. He will bring glory to me by taking from what is mine and making it known to you. . . .

The Spirit searches all things, even the deep things of God. For who among men knows the thoughts of a man except the man's spirit within him? In the same way no one knows the thoughts of God except the Spirit of God.

We have not received the spirit of the world but the Spirit who is from God, *that we may understand what God has freely given us.*

This is what we speak, not in words taught us by human wisdom but in words taught by the Spirit, expressing spiritual truths in spiritual words.

The man without the Spirit does not accept the things that come from the Spirit of God, for they are foolishness to him, and he cannot understand them, because they are spiritually discerned.

The spiritual man makes judgments about all things, but he himself is not subject to any man's judgment.

When the Spirit of the living God dwells inside you, you're a whole lot smarter than you think.

Scripture

John 16:13-14;
1 Corinthians 2:10b-15

✧ DEFINING MOMENTS

That ocean of relief and refreshment that you felt as you turned your back on sin and turned your life over to Jesus Christ's control was the Holy Spirit of God rushing into your heart, filling you with the raw power of everlasting life. The Bible says: "Having believed, you were marked in him [in God] with a seal, the promised Holy Spirit, who is a deposit guaranteeing our inheritance" (Eph. 1:13b-14). Sort of like earnest money on the house God's building you in heaven.

Once we get there, we'll under-stand all that our salvation means. We'll see why we had to go through some of the tough times we faced on earth. Maybe we'll even find out how God pulled off that Red Sea thing, or why He thought it best to put our big nose right in the middle of our face.

But until then, God has given us His Spirit, so that we don't have to rely on our own vague observations and knowledge about spiritual things in order to do what He wants, to understand His plans for us, to put ourselves into position to serve Him with power and freedom.

> "There is no one who magnifies Christ as the Holy Spirit does. His most intense desire is to reveal Jesus Christ to men."
>
> —R. A. Torrey

NEXT UP 🌱 *Oh—by the way—along with the gift of the Holy Spirit comes your own custom-made package of spiritual gifts, which can take you far beyond your natural abilities.*

Did I Do That?

Spiritual Gifts

You already had a nice little handful of talents before you came to God. But look at you now.

 But to each one of us grace has been given as Christ apportioned it. . . .

It was he who gave some to be apostles, some to be prophets, some to be evangelists, and some to be pastors and teachers, to prepare God's people for works of service, so that the body of Christ may be built up until we all reach unity in the faith and in the knowledge of the Son of God and become mature, attaining to the whole measure of the fullness of Christ. . . .

From him the whole body, joined and held together by every supporting ligament, grows and builds itself up in love, as each part does its work. . . .

We have different gifts, according to the grace given us. If a man's gift is prophesying, let him use it in proportion to his faith.

If it is serving, let him serve; if it is teaching, let him teach; if it is encouraging, let him encourage; if it is contributing to the needs of others, let him give generously; if it is leadership, let him govern diligently; if it is showing mercy, let him do it cheerfully. . . .

All these are the work of one and the same Spirit, and he gives them to each one, just as he determines.

Scripture

Ephesians 4:7, 11-13, 16;
Romans 12:6-8; 1 Corinthians 12:11

⤺ DEFINING MOMENTS

God made you with an inborn set of natural abilities, things that have just always come easily to you. Maybe you have a nice singing voice or a flair for calligraphy. Maybe you're good with numbers or can fix anything on wheels. You've trained these abilities, honed them. But the raw materials and understanding were built into your natural makeup. They are gifts from God in every sense of the word.

> "Every member of the Body has the potential to be—and should be led and fed toward functioning as—a fully equipped agent of Jesus Christ."
>
> —Jack Hayford

Now that you've become a Christian, though, God has given you an extra set of gifts—spiritual gifts—to equip you to play the vital role He's given you in His church. Where natural gifts may dictate the kind of work you've chosen, the hobbies you enjoy, or the subjects you like most in school, spiritual gifts are designed to activate your field of ministry. They supercharge you with un-natural abilities to give, to comfort, to challenge, or to speak with boldness. They won't take the place of the things you do well, but they will open up new vistas of opportunity and responsibility—for you to be all that God created you to be.

NEXT UP *God has given you an indescribable gift and the incredible experience of living in His power. But Christianity isn't all about receiving. Are you ready to give it all?*

Counting the Cost

The High Price of Commitment

God is love and peace and joy and contentment. But He is serious business. You'd better be, too.

 "Anyone who does not carry his cross and follow me cannot be my disciple.

"Suppose one of you wants to build a tower. Will he not first sit down and estimate the cost to see if he has enough money to complete it? For if he lays the foundation and is not able to finish it, everyone who sees it will ridicule him, saying, 'This fellow began to build and was not able to finish.'

"Or suppose a king is about to go to war against another king. Will he not first sit down and consider whether he is able with ten thousand men to oppose the one coming against him with twenty thousand? If he is not able, he will send a delegation while the other is still a long way off and will ask for terms of peace.

"In the same way, any of you who does not give up everything he has cannot be my disciple.

"Salt is good, but if it loses its saltiness, how can it be made salty again? . . ."

"*If anyone would come after me, he must deny himself* and take up his cross daily and follow me. For whoever wants to save his life will lose it, but whoever loses his life for me will save it."

Scripture

Luke 14:27-34; 9:23-24

৬ DEFINING MOMENTS

Being a Christian means everything. Everything you are, everything you have. That's why the most miserable people in the world are Christians who aren't willing to take it all the way.

To them, church is uncomfortable, because it keeps confronting them with their sins. Sin is uncomfortable, because the Spirit's taken all the guiltless fun out of it. Relationships are uncomfortable, because being a Christian in one place and a heathen in another makes life hard to keep up with. The call of God stirs their heart, but the call of the world purrs even louder. So with feet in two worlds, they know only the worst of each—the empty promises of sin and the nagging pain of an awakened conscience.

Wow. And they thought God's ways were hard.

The road to the good life is narrow. And pretty steep in a lot of places. But the view is breathtaking—the experiences, unforgettable. And those who choose to walk it find everything their heart desires.

Everything.

> "God nowhere tells us to give up things for the sake of giving them up. He tells us to give them up for the sake of the only thing worth having."
>
> —Oswald Chambers

NEXT UP *You'll find many of the basic, everyday disciplines of Christian living new and challenging, but get good at them. They are spiritual habits you'll never outgrow.*

Notes

SECTION 2

Building on the Basics

Real freedom isn't won by ignoring the rules, but by obeying
them so faithfully that they become second nature.
Like a great symphony musician, you'll find freedom in
your Christian life—not by lazily skipping practice—but by
perfecting the basics, mastering the fundamentals . . . till your
instincts become His, till His will becomes yours.

Called Meetings

Spending Set-Aside Time with God

The moments you spend with no one else but God build the best foundation to a Christian's day.

Give ear to my words, O Lord, consider my sighing. Listen to my cry for help, my King and my God, for to you I pray.

In the morning, O Lord, you hear my voice; in the morning I lay my requests before you and wait in expectation.

You are not a God who takes pleasure in evil; with you the wicked cannot dwell.

The arrogant cannot stand in your presence; you hate all who do wrong. You destroy those who tell lies; bloodthirsty and deceitful men the Lord abhors. But I, by your great mercy, will come into your house; in reverence will I bow down toward your holy temple.

Lead me, O Lord, in your righteousness because of my enemies—make straight your way before me.

Not a word from their mouth can be trusted; their heart is filled with destruction. Their throat is an open grave; with their tongue they speak deceit. . . .

But let all who take refuge in you be glad; let them ever sing for joy. Spread your protection over them, that those who love your name may rejoice in you.

For surely, O Lord, you bless the righteous; you surround them with your favor as with a shield.

Scripture
Psalm 5:1-9, 11-12

⚡ DEFINING MOMENTS

Don't expect your quiet time to come along quietly, because you can usually tell how important something is to your Christian walk by watching how hard Satan works to prevent you from doing it.

Yet if there's one thing you need as a growing believer, it's the early-established, hard-fought discipline of starting each day with your head in the clouds . . . the clouds of God's presence.

Jesus did. The Bible says that He "often withdrew to lonely places and prayed" (Luke 5:16). "Very early in the morning, while it was still dark, Jesus got up, left the house and went off to a solitary place" (Mark 1:35). Not that your time alone with God has to be in the morning, but most of us have learned that leaving quiet time off till bedtime usually results in leaving it off altogether, or at least changes it from a season of refreshed commitments and confident resolve into a weepy, discouraging rehash of the messes you've made that day.

You'll make time for what matters. And this matters the most.

> "If you meet the Lord before you meet anyone else, you'll be pointed in the right direction for whatever comes."
>
> —Elisabeth Elliot

NEXT UP *Hope you're ready to carve out a spot in your day that's earmarked for just you and God to enjoy together. But what are you supposed to fill up a quiet time with?*

Note

Completely Booked

Reading Your Bible

The surest way to God's heart is through His Word. When you start there, you'll never go wrong.

The law of the Lord is perfect, reviving the soul. The statutes of the Lord are trustworthy, making wise the simple.

The precepts of the Lord are right, giving joy to the heart. The commands of the Lord are radiant, giving light to the eyes.

The fear of the Lord is pure, enduring forever. The ordinances of the Lord are sure and altogether righteous.

They are more precious than gold, than much pure gold. . . .

Continue in what you have learned and have become convinced of, because you know those from whom you learned it, and how from infancy you have known the holy Scriptures, which are able to make you wise for salvation through faith in Christ Jesus.

All Scripture is God-breathed and is useful for teaching, rebuking, correcting and training in righteousness, so that the man of God may be thoroughly equipped for every good work. . . .

For the word of God is living and active. Sharper than any double-edged sword, it penetrates even to dividing soul and spirit, joints and marrow; it judges the thoughts and attitudes of the heart.

Scripture

Psalm 19:7-10; 2 Timothy 3:16-17; Hebrews 4:12

DEFINING MOMENTS

The Bible sure is a big book, isn't it? And if you try starting logically at page 1 and barreling straight through to the end, you're likely to bog down somewhere in Leviticus or Numbers, not quite sure how the cleansing ritual for leprosy is going to factor into your life.

So start by reading one of the foundational books of the Bible—like the Gospel of John, or Paul's Letter to the Romans, or the Books of Psalms and Proverbs. If you want to tackle more, you could set off on a journey through the New Testament, starting with Matthew. Read as much as you can, but only as much as you can understand, not being afraid to read only a verse or two a day as long as you mingle it with prayer that God will use it to shine His truth into your life.

> "The Bible gives us heart and hope to make earth like heaven, and to make our hearts and homes a habitation for Christ."
>
> —A. T. Robertson

As you read, you'll begin picking up hints of what God's nature is like, plus new understandings of the Bible's overall message. Little by little—but quicker than you think—you'll start developing a mind that thinks like God thinks, because you know what God says.

NEXT UP *Still, you're likely to forget a lot of what you read if that's all you do with the Scripture. To really let it sink in deep, you've got to lock it away for safekeeping.*

Get It Through Your Head

Scripture Memory

Everybody thinks that memorizing Bible verses is too hard for them, too much trouble. Forget that.

 How can a young man keep his way pure? By living according to your word.

I seek you with all my heart; do not let me stray from your commands.

I have hidden your word in my heart that I might not sin against you. . . .

With my lips I recount all the laws that come from your mouth.

I rejoice in following your statutes as one rejoices in great riches. I meditate on your precepts and consider your ways. I delight in your decrees; I will not neglect your word. . . . Your decrees are the theme of my song wherever I lodge. In the night I remember your name, O Lord, and I will keep your law. . . . If your law had not been my delight, I would have perished in my affliction. I will never forget your precepts, for by them you have preserved my life. Save me, for I am yours; I have sought out your precepts. . . . Your promises have been thoroughly tested, and your servant loves them. . . . Trouble and distress have come upon me, but your commands are my delight.

Scripture

Psalm 119:9-11, 13-16, 54-55, 92-94, 140, 143

DEFINING MOMENTS

You're going to be memorizing something. Either it's song lyrics, or Oscar nominations, or Mark Maguire's home run totals. You're going to be paying enough attention to some interesting aspect of life that the minutest details will become common knowledge to you.

Know what, though? This time next year, you'll have a hard time remembering who even played in the last three Super Bowls, though at the time they seemed so important. You'll forget who your state senator beat in the previous election, though at the time you devoured every article on the race. You'll lose track of the TV story line that used to keep you awake nights trying to figure out what was going to happen next week.

> "One of the primary reasons for studying the Bible is to provide Him with the Word to bring to our remembrance—when we need it."
>
> —Evelyn Christenson

"But the Counselor, the Holy Spirit, whom the Father will send in my name, will teach you all things and will remind you of everything I have said to you" (John 14:26). If, instead of filling your mind with forgettable facts, you load up on the words of life, you place within constant retrieval the right word for every situation.

NEXT UP *Right along with letting the Bible become a staple in your daily diet, prayer will open your life to ongoing fellowship with God. And keep you going all day long.*

Anytime, Anyplace

Prayer

Developing an attitude of prayer will change you from an aimless wanderer to a mighty warrior.

Then Jesus told his disciples a parable to show them that they should always pray and not give up. He said: "In a certain town there was a judge who neither feared God nor cared about men. And there was a widow in that town who kept coming to him with the plea, 'Grant me justice against my adversary.'

"For some time he refused. But finally he said to himself, 'Even though I don't fear God or care about men, yet because this widow keeps bothering me, I will see that she gets justice, so that she won't eventually wear me out with her coming!'"

And the Lord said . . . "Will not God bring about justice for his chosen ones, who cry out to him day and night? Will he keep putting them off? I tell you, he will see that they get justice, and quickly. . . ."

This is the confidence we have in approaching God: that *if we ask anything according to his will, he hears us*. And if we know that he hears us—whatever we ask—we know that we have what we asked of him. . . .

"Ask and it will be given to you; seek and you will find; knock and the door will be opened to you."

Scripture

Luke 18:1-8; 1 John 5:14-15; Matthew 7:7

Notes

DEFINING MOMENTS

Praying comes to us pretty naturally when we accidentally start a grease fire on the stove or get caught out on the lake in a lightning storm. But those who only know the number to God's 911 hotline are missing out on the simple pleasure of picking up the phone anytime they feel like it—day or night, weekends or holidays—and sharing their hearts with someone who always has the time to listen.

Prayer is so many things and can take so many forms. It can be repeating a Bible verse that thanks God for His mercy or reassures you of His faithfulness. It can be your usual laundry list of family members and friends who need God's touch so much. It can be a request, a praise. A smile, a tear. Eyes closed, eyes open. Just you and Him.

So begin committing yourself to the practice of prayer—even when things are going smoothly, even when you feel like you've got everything under control. In prayer, He will lead you by the hand into His very presence and walk beside you every step of the way.

> "The powers of the eternal world have been placed at prayer's disposal. It is the essence of true religion, the channel of all blessings."
>
> —Andrew Murray

NEXT UP *Prayer helps you put your thoughts into words, to sense the deep love of the Father. But journaling makes sure your conversation doesn't disappear into thin air.*

Diary of a Destiny

Keeping a Journal

Trust the ones who've walked this way before. You'll be so glad you kept a record of your journey.

When I was in distress, I sought the Lord; at night I stretched out untiring hands and my soul refused to be comforted.

I remembered you, O God, and I groaned; I mused, and my spirit grew faint. You kept my eyes from closing; I was too troubled to speak.

I thought about the former days, the years of long ago; I remembered my songs in the night.

My heart mused and my spirit inquired: "Will the Lord reject forever? Will he never show his favor again?

"Has his unfailing love vanished forever? Has his promise failed for all time?

"Has God forgotten to be merciful? Has he in anger withheld his compassion?"

Then I thought, "To this I will appeal: the years of the right hand of the Most High."

I will remember the deeds of the Lord; yes, I will remember your miracles of long ago.

I will meditate on all your works and consider all your mighty deeds.

Your ways, O God, are holy. What god is so great as our God?

Scripture

Psalm 77:2-13

DEFINING MOMENTS

When life is right on top of you, when you're wrestling with every detail of your current concerns and troubles, it's hard to imagine a day in the future when you won't be able to recall the way you feel right now or remember how difficult this certain decision was. More importantly, it seems impossible that you won't reflect on how God met you in your misery, pulling you through at the last minute, in ways you never expected.

But that day will come. And with it another new challenge, perhaps different but no less imposing, no less complex than the situation before.

> "Informed by the past, we can speak to God with specific hopes for the future, and with certain assurances about the present."
>
> —Welton Gaddy

Then one morning, your stomach in a knot, you'll pull out your personal journal, flip to a page dated two or three years back, and be suddenly transported to another time and place, to another crossroads conflict that seemed so huge at the time. Wow, you'd almost forgotten about it. Look how desperate you were. Feel the pain in your words. And remember the faithfulness of God—the God who's still here, to deal with the pressure that's so fresh today. Don't you feel better now?

NEXT UP *Worship looks as good in your weekday outfits as it does in your Sunday clothes. Praising God through the day will dress up the way you think, act, and feel.*

All Eyes on Him

Praise and Worship

Wish you had the words to thank God for all He's done for you? You'll find them when you worship.

 Praise the Lord, O my soul; all my inmost being, praise his holy name.

Praise the Lord, O my soul, and forget not all his benefits—who forgives all your sins and heals all your diseases, who redeems your life from the pit and crowns you with love and compassion, who satisfies your desires with good things so that your youth is renewed like the eagle's. . . .

The Lord is compassionate and gracious, slow to anger, abounding in love.

He will not always accuse, nor will he harbor his anger forever; he does not treat us as our sins deserve or repay us according to our iniquities.

For as high as the heavens are above the earth, so great is his love for those who fear him; as far as the east is from the west, so far has he removed our transgressions from us. . . .

From everlasting to everlasting the Lord's love is with those who fear him, and his righteousness with their children's children—with those who keep his covenant and remember to obey his precepts. . . .

Praise the Lord, all his works everywhere in his dominion. Praise the Lord, O my soul.

Scripture

Psalm 103:1-5, 8-12, 17-18, 22

ᒼ DEFINING MOMENTS

Let's face it. We're stuck on ourselves. Worried about the size of our cut in the bonus plan. Dying to get noticed for our part in the project. Hoping nobody wants the last piece of bread in the basket.

That's why worship is so important in the Christian's life, because it goes against the grain of our deep affection for ourselves. When we kick back our head in praise, when we lift our eyes away from the work of our own hands, we cross the bridge into another world. We see things the way they really are—God, in all His awesome glory, in perfect, patient control over everything that touches us. We see the source behind our strength, the provider of each penny,

> "When we are empowered by worship, our day-to-day lives at home, at work, and at leisure take on a new dimension. They rise to the new life."
>
> —Robert Webber

the fount of every blessing. We see Him fully aware of every need, ready and able to meet us at the exact moment we need an answer—this God who knows us so well, yet loves us so much. If there was ever a cure for selfishness, it's the prescription-strength power that flows when we empty ourselves of cares and conceit and lose our grip in the face of His greatness.

NEXT UP *Get ready for something that's gone out of style in the mad dash of modern life—the sweet simplicity of a quiet moment to think, to read, to pray, to go deeper with God.*

Peace, Be Still

Meditation and Quietude

There's a quiet place beyond the buzz of the TV and the telephone. And God's saving you a seat.

 Delight yourself in the Lord and he will give you the desires of your heart.

Commit your way to the Lord; trust in him and he will do this: He will make your righteousness shine like the dawn, the justice of your cause like the noonday sun.

Be still before the Lord and wait patiently for him; do not fret when men succeed in their ways, when they carry out their wicked schemes. . . .

Wait for the Lord and keep his way. He will exalt you to inherit the land; when the wicked are cut off, you will see it.

I have seen a wicked and ruthless man flourishing like a green tree in its native soil, but he soon passed away and was no more; though I looked for him, he could not be found.

Consider the blameless, observe the upright; there is a future for the man of peace.

But all sinners will be destroyed; the future of the wicked will be cut off.

The salvation of the righteous comes from the Lord; he is their stronghold in time of trouble.

The Lord helps them and delivers them; he delivers them from the wicked and saves them, because they take refuge in him.

Scripture

Psalm 37:4-7, 34-40

Notes

DEFINING MOMENTS

The New Agers came in, started talking about focusing and finding their center (and stuff like that), and made people think of meditation as some heebie-jeebie, hippie holdover that feels at home on a PBS special, but not on our living room sofas.

Just because someone misuses God's gift, however, doesn't diminish its importance. Meditation is a much-needed Christian discipline. When you seek a silent place away from the pull of the newspaper or the approaching drumbeats of a work deadline, when you feast on a single verse of the Scripture, letting the Holy Spirit bring to your mind new lessons to learn, new twists on the truth, new insights to gather . . . you will learn to recognize God's voice and grow in your relationship.

> "We must carefully plan solitude. We do not take the spiritual life seriously if we do not set aside some time to be with, and listen to, God."
>
> —Henri Nouwen

You don't have to go out looking for demands and distractions. They'll find you—enough to fill every second of your life with noise and activity, yet still leave you restless and dissatisfied. Come quietly before God. Meditate on His Word. And enjoy His satisfying rest.

NEXT UP *Now we're getting somewhere. The next step in growing as a Christian is learning how to keep your life an open book before God, and let nothing come between you.*

Out in the Open

Confession and Repentance

Nobody expects you to be perfect. But by owning up to your mistakes, you get a whole lot closer to it.

He who conceals his sins does not prosper, but whoever confesses and renounces them finds mercy.

Blessed is the man who always fears the Lord, but he who hardens his heart falls into trouble. . . .

If we claim to have fellowship with him yet walk in the darkness, we lie and do not live by the truth. But if we walk in the light, as he is in the light, we have fellowship with one another, and the blood of Jesus, his Son, purifies us from all sin. If we claim to be without sin, we deceive ourselves and the truth is not in us. *If we confess our sins, he is faithful and just and will forgive us* our sins and purify us from all unrighteousness. . . .

For we do not have a high priest who is unable to sympathize with our weaknesses, but we have one who has been tempted in every way, just as we are—yet was without sin.

Let us then approach the throne of grace with confidence, so that we may receive mercy and find grace to help us in our time of need.

Scripture

Proverbs 28:13-14; 1 John 1:6-9; Hebrews 4:5-16

Notes

DEFINING MOMENTS

God is no pushover. His call to holy living is very clear, very firm, very hard to misunderstand. Let's not trick ourselves into thinking that His heart of compassion has made Him soft on sin.

But rest in this: "He remembers that we are dust" (Ps. 103:14). He knows where we've come from. He understands the bad habits we've molded over the years, the comfortable corners we run to when we're tired or upset or discouraged. Truth is, the anger we feel pressing down on us is more ours than His, for while we could kick ourselves for caving again, He's heartbroken that we've sold ourselves out so cheaply, that we've chosen the path of pain when He has offered us the path of peace.

> "Christianity is strange. It orders man to acknowledge that he is evil, even abominable. Yet it also bids him to be like God."
>
> —Blaise Pascal

So as you catch yourself in compromise, confess your mistake. And promise (with God's help) that you'll turn your back on this foolishness. Confession gets your sin out in front where you can deal with it. Repentance takes it out to the curb where God can haul it off with the rest of your garbage. And leave you feeling clean again.

NEXT UP *God hasn't saved you just so you could enjoy life in a better mood. He has placed you in a community of faith, where your little part can be multiplied in ministry.*

Strength in Numbers

Why You Belong in Church

Lone Rangers look pretty tough on the big screen. But underneath, they're nothing but palefaces.

The body is a unit, though it is made up of many parts; and though all its parts are many, they form one body. So it is with Christ. . . .

If the foot should say, "Because I am not a hand, I do not belong to the body," it would not for that reason cease to be part of the body. And if the ear should say, "Because I am not an eye, I do not belong to the body," it would not for that reason cease to be part of the body.

If the whole body were an eye, where would the sense of hearing be? If the whole body were an ear, where would the sense of smell be? But in fact God has arranged the parts in the body, every one of them, just as he wanted them to be. If they were all one part, where would the body be? *As it is, there are many parts, but one body. . . .*

But God has combined the members of the body and has given greater honor to the parts that lacked it, so that there should be no division in the body, but that its parts should have equal concern for each other.

If one part suffers, every part suffers with it; if one part is honored, every part rejoices with it.

Scripture

1 Corinthians 12:12, 15-20, 24b-26

DEFINING MOMENTS

Your week may be filled with sales meetings and lunch plans, with night classes and homework, with diapers and runny noses. Whatever ordinary means to you. You may be having a squabble with your sister or a hassle with your landlord. You may be knee deep in credit card bills or trying not to worry about that curious new pain in your side.

The week has a way of wearing you down, of hitting you head-on with more troubles and temptations than you were hoping to handle. You can fall into bed on Saturday night a limp rag. A sigh. A surrender. You may feel almost as far out of God's plan as you were before you gave your life to Him.

> "It's only as we, as a body of Christians, grow together in Jesus Christ that we will truly reflect faith, hope, and love."
>
> —Gene Getz

But no matter what your week's been like, you can walk into God's house on Sunday morning and know that you're right where you're supposed to be—that you're part of something bigger than yourself, a place where you belong, a member of an eternal family. You need them, and they need you. And together, you can find the strength to face another week. To go on another day.

NEXT UP *More than Sunday morning, though, you need a face-to-face connection with a few close Christian friends who can help to keep you living what you say you believe.*

Between Friends

Accountability

God can help you be the person you want to be. But seek out somebody who'll help you see to it.

The Lord sent Nathan to David. When he came to him, he said, "There were two men in a certain town, one rich and the other poor.

"The rich man had a very large number of sheep and cattle, but the poor man had nothing except one little ewe lamb he had bought. He raised it, and it grew up with him and his children. It shared his food, drank from his cup and even slept in his arms. It was like a daughter to him.

"Now a traveler came to the rich man, but the rich man refrained from taking one of his own sheep or cattle to prepare a meal for the traveler who had come to him. Instead, he took the ewe lamb that belonged to the poor man and prepared it for the one who had come to him. . . ."

Then Nathan said to David, "You are the man! . . . Why did you despise the word of the Lord by doing what is evil in his eyes? You struck down Uriah the Hittite with the sword and took his wife to be your own. You killed him with the sword of the Ammonites. . . .

"You did it in secret, but I will do this thing in broad daylight before all Israel."

Then David said to Nathan, "I have sinned against the Lord."

Scripture

2 Samuel 12:1-4, 7, 9, 12-13

Notes

DEFINING MOMENTS

"I will praise the Lord who counsels me; even at night my heart instructs me. I have set the Lord always before me" (Psalm 16:7-8).

He's there. Wherever you are. Whatever you're feeling. Without having to play a silly mind game or pretend something that's not real, you can just believe the fact that God is always with you, His power always within reach, His help always one word away.

But when it's late, when you've had a tough day, when a drink is sounding awfully good or the remote control is driving through a bad section of TV-land, the features on God's face can dim a little. His invisible presence can fade into your forgetfulness.

> "I believe if a man gets close to a true spiritual champion, he will become one. We become like the people we associate with."
>
> —Ronnie Floyd

But if you've got a couple of friends you've promised to stay accountable to, if you dread the thought of facing them without a clear conscience and a good word of testimony, you can flash their faces through your mind or make a quick phone call and remember what a holy life is worth.

Look, we're all in this thing together.

NEXT UP *You've made some good friends by joining the family of faith, but also some sworn enemies. Let's look at who's out to get you and what it's going to take to win.*

SEC3TION

Sizing Up the Enemy

Any good ballplayer will tell you that half the price of victory
is taking time to know your opponent—to analyze his tenden-
cies, his strategies, the way he reacts in certain situations.
Victory in your Christian life is a lot like that. Oh, the
power's on your side, but you need to know what you're up
against. Now get out there and win.

Sweat the Small Stuff

Subtle Sins

You may have to go out looking for the biggies. But the littlest sins can cause you the most trouble.

But among you there must not be even a hint of sexual immorality, or of any kind of impurity, or of greed, because these are improper for God's holy people. Nor should there be obscenity, foolish talk or coarse joking, which are out of place, but rather thanksgiving.

For of this you can be sure: No immoral, impure or greedy person—such a man is an idolater—has any inheritance in the kingdom of Christ and of God. Let no one deceive you with empty words, for because of such things God's wrath comes on those who are disobedient. Therefore do not be partners with them. . . .

Be very careful, then, how you live—not as unwise but as wise, making the most of every opportunity, because the days are evil.

Therefore do not be foolish, but understand what the Lord's will is. Do not get drunk on wine, which leads to debauchery. Instead, be filled with the Spirit.

Speak to one another with psalms, hymns and spiritual songs. Sing and make music in your heart to the Lord, always giving thanks to God the Father for everything, in the name of our Lord Jesus Christ.

Scripture
Ephesians 5:3-7, 15-20

↫ DEFINING MOMENTS

Ever tried cleaning up a room that was totally trashed? When the dresser drawers won't shut and the bed disguises an unseen colony of clothes and clutter—when the last shoe has finally dropped and you've been surrounded by the law of gravity—it's time to do the big stuff first. The glaring things. The obvious things. Like making your bed. Folding up your sweaters. Returning all the plates, forks, and glasses to the kitchen.

> "The light Jesus brings helps us to see ourselves more clearly and not to be fooled by what is hidden inside."
>
> —James Houston

But underneath the chief culprits lies a second layer of vandals. Dust. Corners. Baseboards. Pockets of disarray you didn't notice before, but now—with all the major problems taken care of—they cry out for correction. On and on it goes. The light exposes another. You fix, tinker, and straighten. You want to be clean.

As a growing Christian, you need to stay constantly open to the white glove of God's Word—not to keep you endlessly frustrated with your faults, but to keep unseen sins from becoming an all-day mess. What's under the rug can be more of a problem than you think.

NEXT UP ↝ *Becoming a Christian doesn't automatically eliminate the bad habits you've formed over the years. But it does give you power to overcome them, one try at a time.*

Familiar Places

Bad Habits

Every habit opens a window for Satan to climb in again. But God has a way for you to shut him out.

For we know that our old self was crucified with him so that the body of sin might be done away with, that we should no longer be slaves to sin—because anyone who has died has been freed from sin.

Now if we died with Christ, we believe that we will also live with him. For we know that since Christ was raised from the dead, he cannot die again; death no longer has mastery over him. The death he died, he died to sin once for all; but the life he lives, he lives to God.

In the same way, *count yourselves dead to sin but alive to God in Christ Jesus.* Therefore do not let sin reign in your mortal body so that you obey its evil desires.

Do not offer the parts of your body to sin, as instruments of wickedness, but rather offer yourselves to God, as those who have been brought from death to life; and offer the parts of your body to him as instruments of righteousness. For sin shall not be your master, because you are not under law, but under grace. . . .

You have been set free from sin and have become slaves to righteousness.

Scripture

Romans 6:6-14, 18

᧐ **DEFINING MOMENTS**

Every time you've turned to an old familiar, forbidden place for relief or revenge, every time you've reacted without thinking or given in when you should have toughed it out, you've unwittingly widened the entrance ramp onto the easy street of compromise. You've made it that much easier to come back for a return trip next time the urge strikes and to keep your car in the straight and narrow.

That's what habits are—really wide, open highways you can drive with your eyes closed. Roads you've traveled so many times that you anticipate every bend, every bump. But you know better than anybody else that you have no business being out there. And if you just had the strength, you'd whip that car around right now and head back where it's safe.

So do it, because now your no has the power of God behind it. And every time you lean hard into His side for the strength to resist, you close another entrance ramp. You shut down another access road. You play dead to the call of the highway. You win over habitual sin.

> "Being free from sin not only means I can be strong in Him to stop doing wrong. It also means in Him I have the ability to do what's right."
>
> —Stuart Briscoe

NEXT UP *Taking on tough customers like these with the power of prayer and the truth of God's Word will get you ready to tackle any temptation—even when it slips in unnoticed.*

Notes

Sucker Punches

Temptation

Consider it pure joy, my brothers, whenever you face trials of many kinds, because you know that the testing of your faith develops perseverance. Perseverance must finish its work so that you may be mature and complete, not lacking anything. . . .

Blessed is the man who perseveres under trial, because when he has stood the test, he will receive the crown of life that God has promised to those who love him.

When tempted, no one should say, "God is tempting me." For God cannot be tempted by evil, nor does he tempt anyone; but each one is tempted when, by his own evil desire, he is dragged away and enticed. Then, after desire has conceived, it gives birth to sin; and sin, when it is full-grown, gives birth to death.

Don't be deceived, my dear brothers. . . .

So, if you think you are standing firm, be careful that you don't fall! No temptation has seized you except what is common to man. And God is faithful; *he will not let you be tempted beyond what you can bear.* But when you are tempted, he will also provide a way out so that you can stand up under it.

> Temptation can strike when you least expect it. But it's only as strong as the time you waste on it.

Scripture

James 1:2-4, 12-16;
1 Corinthians 10:12-13

Notes

♻ DEFINING MOMENTS

Satan didn't sleep through your salvation experience. Your sudden departure from the kingdom of darkness into the kingdom of light sent off warning flares in his security division. He set a strategic plan in motion to make sure your faith gets lost on its way to your lifestyle.

So never underestimate the depths of his deceit. He knows a lot about you, for sure. But we know a few things about him.

For one, we know that God has limited the reach of Satan's temptations. The devil may hold the night stick, but God holds the leash. And God can even turn those schemes to your advantage, using them to toughen muscles in your character and open your eyes to places where you're trusting self instead of trusting God.

> "The devil knows that if he can get our minds to dwell on certain sins, then it will be just a matter of time before those sins are acted out."
>
> —Greg Laurie

Remember, too, that temptation isn't sin. It just feels like it. And nowhere in the whole process are you forced to comply—even if you're not quick enough to douse the first flicker of Satan's finesse.

He can quicken your own desire. But he can't make you do anything. Don't believe a word he says.

NEXT UP *But no matter how hard you try, even though you know God's forgiven you, you still carry the guilt of things you've done in the past. Where does that go to die?*

It's All Behind You

Overcoming Past Guilt

You've been forgiven. But you can't forget. And at times you wonder if you'll ever get past your past.

Therefore, *there is now no condemnation for those who are in Christ Jesus*, because through Christ Jesus the law of the Spirit of life set me free from the law of sin and death.

For what the law was powerless to do in that it was weakened by the sinful nature, God did by sending his own Son in the likeness of sinful man to be a sin offering. And so he condemned sin in sinful man, in order that the righteous requirements of the law might be fully met in us, who do not live according to the sinful nature but according to the Spirit. . . .

For you did not receive a spirit that makes you a slave again to fear, but you received the Spirit of sonship. And by him we cry, "Abba, Father. . . ."

What, then, shall we say in response to this? If God is for us, who can be against us? He who did not spare his own Son, but gave him up for us all—how will he not also, along with him, graciously give us all things?

Who will bring any charge against those whom God has chosen? It is God who justifies.

Who is he that condemns? Christ Jesus, who died—more than that, who was raised to life—is at the right hand of God and is also interceding for us.

Scripture

Romans 8:1-4, 15, 31-34

⚡ DEFINING MOMENTS

If you only knew how clean your record was. If you could only believe how much the Father loves you.

If you could finally understand that when you gave your heart to Jesus, you "clothed yourself with Christ" (Gal. 3:27), so that when God looks at you now, He doesn't see that junk you used to wear, but the pure, shining garments of Christ's everlasting righteousness.

He sees you for who you really are. A full-fledged child of the living God. Oh, you've still got some wrinkles to iron out. And as you stay open to the Spirit's conviction through the Bible, through sermons, through the words of a true friend, you'll be drawn to new repentance. You'll want to be like Christ no matter what it costs.

> "Through true guilt, the Holy Spirit seeks to draw us closer to God. Through false, incriminating guilt, Satan seeks to separate us from God."
>
> —Jim Henry

But guilt gives itself away by beating you down, by presenting forgiven material into evidence, by accusing you of hypocrisy when God says you're worthy of heaven. Turn the guilt of your past into a testimony of God's power. And walk away with your head in the clouds.

NEXT UP *When your faith is young and exuberance spills over easily into life, some people won't be crazy about who you're becoming. You'd be crazy to listen to them.*

Critic's Corner

Other People's Perceptions

Lots of people may have lots of opinions about you. But you're only playing for an audience of One.

Who is going to harm you if you are eager to do good? But even if you should suffer for what is right, you are blessed. "Do not fear what they fear; do not be frightened."

But in your hearts set apart Christ as Lord. Always be prepared to give an answer to everyone who asks you to give the reason for the hope that you have. But do this with gentleness and respect, keeping a clear conscience, so that those who speak maliciously against your good behavior in Christ may be ashamed of their slander. . . .

If you are insulted because of the name of Christ, you are blessed, for the Spirit of glory and of God rests on you.

If you suffer, it should not be as a murderer or thief or any other kind of criminal, or even as a meddler. However, if you suffer as a Christian, do not be ashamed, but praise God that you bear that name. For it is time for judgment to begin with the family of God; and if it begins with us, what will the outcome be for those who do not obey the gospel of God? . . .

So then, those who suffer according to God's will should commit themselves to their faithful Creator and continue to do good.

Scripture

1 Peter 3:13-16; 4:14-17, 19

⚡ DEFINING MOMENTS

May as well be on the lookout for a couple of thieves who like to prey on new Christians who are serious about being Christlike.

One is the old friend who liked you better the way you were, back when you were a lot more open to having a good time and going to church didn't interfere with every weekend.

The other one is the Christian who's seen your kind come along before and liked you better when you were still a prayer request. Now you're a ball of fire who's just crazy enough to take what you read in the Bible at face value, who thinks there's nothing God can't do through people who pray and churches who love each other. Your enthusiasm threatens them. They're supposed to be the ones helping you.

> "Conformity is a joy thief, but fixing our eyes on Jesus is a joyful, life-giving exercise."
>
> —Ed Young

So if you haven't already, you're sure to start feeling the heat from those who want you either more like the world or more like the status quo. Just keep believing that what the Bible says is true, and keep loving them the way you'd want them to love you.

NEXT UP *One of the biggest enemies in your fight for Christian victory is a foe so small, you could easily overlook it. But it's so close to your heart that it's hard to give up.*

Talk, Talk, Talk, Talk

Your Words

A person's words can tell you a lot about who they really are. What are your words saying about you?

When we put bits into the mouths of horses to make them obey us, we can turn the whole animal. Or take ships as an example. Although they are so large and are driven by strong winds, they are steered by a very small rudder wherever the pilot wants to go.

Likewise *the tongue is a small part of the body, but it makes great boasts.* Consider what a great forest is set on fire by a small spark. The tongue also is a fire, a world of evil among the parts of the body. It corrupts the whole person, sets the whole course of his life on fire, and is itself set on fire by hell.

All kinds of animals, birds, reptiles and creatures of the sea are being tamed and have been tamed by man, but no man can tame the tongue. It is a restless evil, full of deadly poison. With the tongue we praise our Lord and Father, and with it we curse men, who have been made in God's likeness.

Out of the same mouth come praise and cursing. My brothers, this should not be. Can both fresh water and salt water flow from the same spring? My brothers, can a fig tree bear olives, or a grapevine bear figs? Neither can a salt spring produce fresh water.

Scripture

James 3:3-12

Notes

⮎ DEFINING MOMENTS

You didn't mean to say it. It just slipped out. Everybody knows how it feels when the gossip engine is in full swing, when the camaraderie of shared complaints and put-downs makes you say things you promised yourself not to—little tidbits you'd been told in confidence, jokes and jabs you toss out for public enjoyment though you'd never speak them right to someone's face. We all understand.

But knowing that we all understand doesn't make it right. And working harder to bite your lip next time only provides temporary relief. Jesus said that "out of the overflow of the heart the mouth speaks" (Matt. 12:34)—that if we want our words (or our silence) to be pure and pleasing, we must change our attitudes to match.

"Let your words be few, lest you say with your tongue what you will afterward repent with your heart."

—George MacDonald

So . . . want to withstand the urge to sling the next insult? Then try loving the person who irritates you. Want to never make another idle remark at another's expense? Then pray for God to help you want the best for your grouchy neighbor. Kind words come from clean hearts.

NEXT UP *Being new to something (like the Christian life) can make you feel outclassed by those who do it so well. But we're not racing each other. We're racing ourselves.*

Measuring Sticks

Comparing Yourself with Others

We do not dare to classify or compare ourselves with some who commend themselves. When they measure themselves by themselves and compare themselves with themselves, they are not wise.

We, however, will not boast beyond proper limits, but will confine our boasting to the field God has assigned to us, a field that reaches even to you. We are not going too far in our boasting, as would be the case if we had not come to you, for we did get as far as you with the gospel of Christ.

Neither do we go beyond our limits by boasting of work done by others. Our hope is that, as your faith continues to grow, our area of activity among you will greatly expand, so that we can preach the gospel in the regions beyond you. For we do not want to boast about work already done in another man's territory.

But, "Let him who boasts boast in the Lord." For it is not the one who commends himself who is approved, but the one whom the Lord commends. . . .

Each one should test his own actions. Then he can take pride in himself, without comparing himself to somebody else, for each one should carry his own load.

> There are people in your church who are so neat, who have so much to offer. You're one of them.

Scripture

2 Corinthians 10:12-18;
Galatians 6:4-5

⚡ DEFINING MOMENTS

You may feel as though you know next to nothing about Christ. But so did everybody when they first started down this road—even the ones who can pray like they're six inches from heaven or can wow you with their grasp of biblical wisdom and insight. Even the ones who can sing chills down people's spines in a worship service or who rarely step off an airplane without a new convert under each arm.

But for one thing, God's a lot more pleased with folks who are faithful than with those who can draw a crowd.

> "We don't have to fear being inadequate. Our God is adequate. He will provide everything we need to serve Him."
>
> —Chip Ricks

And for another, God's invested time and talents in you that He's just starting to use. And as you yield them to His service—whether you get any recognition or not—you'll begin growing into the ministry He wants you to perform.

God's putting a whole team together in your town or city to take His love and salvation to every person who'll listen. It's going to take all of you working together, combining your callings and pooling your abilities. So start practicing your part. Your piece is important.

NEXT UP *You didn't do anything to earn your salvation; you don't have to pass a test every five years to keep it current. You're in. You're staying in. What's so hard about that?*

Good Enough

Performance-Based Acceptance

> If we all had to work our way into God's good graces, heaven would be one lonely place.

I would like to learn just one thing from you: Did you receive the Spirit by observing the law, or by believing what you heard? Are you so foolish? After beginning with the Spirit, *are you now trying to attain your goal by human effort?* Have you suffered so much for nothing—if it really was for nothing?

Does God give you his Spirit and work miracles among you because you observe the law, or because you believe what you heard? . . .

All who rely on observing the law are under a curse, for it is written: "Cursed is everyone who does not continue to do everything written in the Book of the Law." Clearly no one is justified before God by the law, because, "The righteous will live by faith." The law is not based on faith; on the contrary, "The man who does these things will live by them."

Christ redeemed us from the curse of the law by becoming a curse for us. . . . He redeemed us in order that the blessing given to Abraham might come to the Gentiles through Christ Jesus, so that by faith we might receive the promise of the Spirit.

Scripture

Galatians 3:2-5, 10-14

⸜ DEFINING MOMENTS

Maybe your dad wasn't quick with an "I love you."
Maybe he said the lawn looked pretty good, but that
you could have been a lot more careful around the
flower bed. Maybe he was fairly pleased with your
musical performance, but scolded you for being flat in
a few places. He may have thought
four A's and two B's wasn't too bad.
But it could have been better. You
could have tried harder. You could
have done more. But what you did
was never enough.

> "Grace is the unconditional
> love of God in Christ freely
> given to the sinful, the
> undeserving, and the imperfect."
>
> —David Seamands

So getting up ten minutes early
three days this week to pray and
read your Bible was good. Wasn't it,
Father? Of course, it could have been
more like twenty. And every day.

Giving an extra five dollars in
your tithe check this week was pretty generous. Right,
Father? Or would ten dollars have earned more of a
smile?

Listen, you can always do more to return the favor
God's given. There's not a person alive who can't deep-
en his devotion. But child of God, He loves you and
accepts you right where you are. And you can't work
hard enough to get more. The proof is in His palm.

NEXT UP ⸜ *You're probably not going
to like this next part. And granted, it's an easy
target to pick on. But the things that entertain
you shouldn't be the things Christ died for.*

Badly Exposed

TV, Movies, the Media

What goes for family viewing these days can become one of a Christian's prime-time problems.

I will be careful to lead a blameless life—when will you come to me?

I will walk in my house with blameless heart. I will set before my eyes no vile thing.

The deeds of faithless men I hate; they will not cling to me. Men of perverse heart shall be far from me; I will have nothing to do with evil.

Whoever slanders his neighbor in secret, him will I put to silence; whoever has haughty eyes and a proud heart, him will I not endure.

My eyes will be on the faithful in the land, that they may dwell with me; he whose walk is blameless will minister to me.

No one who practices deceit will dwell in my house; no one who speaks falsely will stand in my presence.

Every morning I will put to silence all the wicked in the land; I will cut off every evildoer from the city of the Lord. . . .

Finally, brothers, whatever is true, whatever is noble, whatever is right, whatever is pure, whatever is lovely, whatever is admirable—if anything is excellent or praiseworthy—think about such things.

Scripture

Psalm 101:2-8; Philippians 4:8

Notes

DEFINING MOMENTS

The problem with TV and the movies is a lot more than demonic aliens, filthy language, and sex on seventy channels. We've been all over those things. They're all terrible. And everybody knows it. We're drawn to them for some sick, sinful reason, but nobody can justify the habit of enjoying that kind of entertainment. Not a single one of us would want to share a sofa with Jesus while that stuff is on the air.

But that's just the beginning of it, because even though we can learn to forego the seedier stuff and turn our tastes to more acceptable fare like documentaries and newsmagazines, game shows and Mayberry reruns, football and tennis matches, we still pay the price of forfeiting huge chunks of our time to what amounts to a mindless escape.

Things that require no thought of us, that fill in every line and complete every question, steal from us the desire to grow and create, to pour ourselves into other people, to listen to God no matter how strange the quietness feels at first. Promise you'll think about it.

> "We cannot afford the luxury of entertaining ourselves with sin if we want to maintain our moral purity."
>
> —Bill and Kathy Peel

NEXT UP *You're sold on Christ and certain you've done the right thing. But sometimes you wonder how you can really be sure. Is that allowed after you've already committed?*

Just Wondering

Doubts and Questions

You can ask God any question, as long as you understand He knows when you need the answer.

Now Thomas (called Didymus), one of the Twelve, was not with the disciples when Jesus came. So the other disciples told him, "We have seen the Lord!" But he said to them, "Unless I see the nail marks in his hands and put my finger where the nails were, and put my hand into his side, I will not believe it."

A week later his disciples were in the house again, and Thomas was with them. Though the doors were locked, Jesus came and stood among them and said, "Peace be with you!" Then he said to Thomas, "Put your finger here; see my hands. Reach out your hand and put it into my side. Stop doubting and believe." Thomas said to him, "My Lord and my God!" Then Jesus told him, "Because you have seen me, you have believed; blessed are those who have not seen and yet have believed. . . ."

This then is how we know that we belong to the truth, and how we set our hearts at rest in his presence whenever our hearts condemn us. *For God is greater than our hearts, and he knows everything. . . .*

Those who obey his commands live in him, and he in them. And this is how we know that he lives in us: We know it by the Spirit he gave us.

Scripture

John 20:24-29;
1 John 3:19-20, 24

DEFINING MOMENTS

You're right. There is a lot to swallow here.

God made the world in six days. Jesus was born to a little virgin teenager. His death on the cross somehow pays the penalty for all your sins if you merely confess your need for it and believe that He's God's Son. The Bible is His Word of truth, even though others claim they have another God and another book and another way to get close to Him.

Makes you wonder.

> "Our loving Heavenly Father desires our presence even if it means pouring out our hearts in anger, frustration, and fear."
>
> —Sandra Glahn

What about good people who die but who didn't go to church much? What about the thirty-five-year-old mother of three who's dying of cancer and trying to prepare her family to live without her? What about the things that aren't going right in your life right now? Does God have any answers for things like these?

Yes. The Bible is full of them. But doubts and questions will always remain. Feel free to ask them anytime. But if you still don't understand, be willing to be satisfied with this: God is good, He knows what's best for you, and you can trust Him. That answers a lot right there.

Notes

 **NEXT UP** *Coming to Christ required only a single thought. But learning to live like Him requires a whole new way of thinking. And it's way different from anybody else's.*

SECTION 4

A New Way of Thinking

God looks at things a little differently than we do. In His kingdom, leaders serve. Givers receive. Those who pour their lives out in service to others find their own cup filled to overflowing. You, too, will grow deeper in Jesus as you start letting your own will take a backseat to His, steering your focus away from what's in it for you.

Whatever You Say

Doing God's Will

Wanting your own way starts early in life. But the sooner you start giving it up, the better off you'll be.

"Therefore I tell you, do not worry about your life, what you will eat or drink; or about your body, what you will wear. Is not life more important than food, and the body more important than clothes? Look at the birds of the air; they do not sow or reap or store away in barns, and yet your heavenly Father feeds them. Are you not much more valuable than they? Who of you by worrying can add a single hour to his life?

"And why do you worry about clothes? See how the lilies of the field grow. They do not labor or spin. Yet I tell you that not even Solomon in all his splendor was dressed like one of these. If that is how God clothes the grass of the field, which is here today and tomorrow is thrown into the fire, will he not much more clothe you, O you of little faith?

"So do not worry, saying, 'What shall we eat?' or 'What shall we drink?' or 'What shall we wear?' For the pagans run after all these things, and your heavenly Father knows that you need them.

But *seek first his kingdom and his righteousness*, and all these things will be given to you as well."

Scripture
Matthew 6:25-33

Notes

ᔐ DEFINING MOMENTS

God has given you the freedom of taking your best stab at life, of spreading out your own map, striking out on your own instincts, and finding your own way to the land of meaning and purpose.

But in case that responsibility leaves you feeling unsettled and ill equipped, He is more than willing to oversee your travel plans, to plot out the routes that He knows are best—no matter how out-of-the-way they may appear to you.

After all, He knows the places where you're likely to bump into lane closures and construction delays. He knows that the squiggly red line on the map that appears to cut nearly an hour off your trip disguises a sea of

> "Until you are ready to make any adjustment necessary to follow and obey what God has said, you will be of little use to God."
>
> —Henry Blackaby

school zones, stop signs, and Friday night ballgame traffic. He even knows they've opened one of your favorite restaurants on a little backroad that you never would have spotted if you'd gone the way you were thinking. With a travel agent like that helping you chart your path through life, why would anybody want to trust their own sense of direction? Would you?

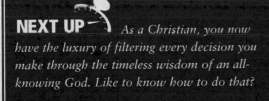

NEXT UP *As a Christian, you now have the luxury of filtering every decision you make through the timeless wisdom of an all-knowing God. Like to know how to do that?*

What a Bargain

Decision Making

Your new lease on life comes with a lifetime option of seeing every decision as an opportunity.

This is what the Sovereign Lord, the Holy One of Israel, says: "In repentance and rest is your salvation, in quietness and trust is your strength, but you would have none of it.

"You said, 'No, we will flee on horses.' Therefore you will flee! You said, 'We will ride off on swift horses.' Therefore your pursuers will be swift!

"A thousand will flee at the threat of one; at the threat of five you will all flee away, till you are left like a flagstaff on a mountaintop, like a banner on a hill."

Yet the Lord longs to be gracious to you; he rises to show you compassion. For the Lord is a God of justice. Blessed are all who wait for him!

O people of Zion, who live in Jerusalem, you will weep no more. How gracious he will be when you cry for help! As soon as he hears, he will answer you.

Although the Lord gives you the bread of adversity and the water of affliction, your teachers will be hidden no more; with your own eyes you will see them.

Whether you turn to the right or to the left, *your ears will hear a voice behind you, saying, "This is the way*; walk in it."

Scripture
Isaiah 30:15-21

Notes

♻ DEFINING MOMENTS

You now have a partner in life. And He is not a silent one. This new Friend who walks beside you into every decision you make has no desire to withhold the guidance you need to arrive at sound, godly decisions. Count on Him to always let you see enough of every situation to make the best choice, whether you're choosing between right and wrong or between good and better. As badly as you want to be faithful to Him, to use your life to bring Him honor, He wants you to know His will. To talk where you can hear.

But you won't always want to listen. You may be too mad to think clearly, too afraid to act boldly, or perhaps just too busy to give Him the time of day. But if you'll strip away any desire for personal gain or attention, if you'll turn to the Bible for truthful instruction, and if you'll quiet yourself before God and allow His Holy Spirit to direct and confirm your thoughts—you'll get your answer. You'll be able to step out in obedient faith, willing to make a mistake as long as you know your heart is right. Good choice.

> "What would be the result if in this city, every church member should begin to do as Jesus would do? It is not easy to go into details of the result."
>
> —Charles Sheldon

NEXT UP → *It's no big surprise that the Christian way of thinking is totally foreign to the worldly mind. But it has to become second nature to you if you're to have any impact.*

The Big Picture

The Christian Worldview

Whether they know it or not, everyone operates from a basic belief system. Get to know yours.

Then Peter, filled with the Holy Spirit, said to them: "Rulers and elders of the people! If we are being called to account today for an act of kindness shown to a cripple and are asked how he was healed, then know this, you and all the people of Israel: It is by the name of Jesus Christ of Nazareth, whom you crucified but whom God raised from the dead, that this man stands before you healed.

"He is 'the stone you builders rejected, which has become the capstone.' "Salvation is found in no one else, for there is no other name under heaven given to men by which we must be saved."

When they saw the courage of Peter and John and realized that they were unschooled, ordinary men, they were astonished and they took note that these men had been with Jesus. . . .

"What are we going to do with these men?" they asked. . . . Then they called them in again and commanded them not to speak or teach at all in the name of Jesus. But Peter and John replied, "Judge for yourselves whether it is right in God's sight to obey you rather than God. For *we cannot help speaking about what we have seen and heard.*"

Scripture

Acts 4:8-13, 16, 18-20

Notes

 DEFINING MOMENTS

Beliefs have consequences, even the ones that people rarely spend time thinking about. Those, in fact, may be the scariest beliefs of all. But whether deliberately or unwittingly, people live their lives based on a set of understood principles. Their answers to the questions of where they came from, what they're doing here, and where they're ultimately headed colors the decisions they make, the work they do, and the responsibility they feel for themselves and others.

They live by what is called a worldview—be it secular and self-centered, humanistic, New Age, or whatever.

So do you. As a holder of the Christian worldview, you have given up your right to mindlessly float through life on the driftwood of someone else's opinions. The Bible's revelation of who God is, what He has done to redeem fallen humanity, and the eternal nature of His heavenly kingdom should affect every position you hold on every possible issue of modern life. To know how to live, you must first know what you believe. Dig in and find out.

> "We need to get our heads out of the secular sand and stop being intimidated by the post-Christian culture that surrounds us."
>
> —Chuck Colson

NEXT UP *Most people do well if they can wait a week to see the fruit of their decisions. But the Christian life doesn't promise to pay off in a hurry—or in the way you think.*

Farsighted

Long-Term Perspective

Remember those earlier days after you had received the light, when you stood your ground in a great contest in the face of suffering. Sometimes you were publicly exposed to insult and persecution; at other times you stood side by side with those who were so treated. You sympathized with those in prison and joyfully accepted the confiscation of your property, because you knew that you yourselves had better and lasting possessions.

So do not throw away your confidence; it will be richly rewarded. You need to persevere so that when you have done the will of God, you will receive what he has promised. For in just a very little while, "He who is coming will come and will not delay. But my righteous one will live by faith. And if he shrinks back, I will not be pleased with him."

But we are not of those who shrink back and are destroyed, but of those who believe and are saved. . . .

I have been crucified with Christ and I no longer live, but Christ lives in me. The life I live in the body, I live by faith in the Son of God, who loved me and gave himself for me.

> You've got forever to see the truth win out, to get your questions answered. Are you willing to wait?

Scripture

Hebrews 10:32-39;
Galatians 2:20

ᘓ **DEFINING MOMENTS**

This is the era of the quick turnaround. If we can't call tonight and have it on our desk first thing in the morning, we'll call someone else who can. That's the way the world thinks. That's the way the world runs. But that's the way you get yourself into trouble if you're expecting God to cater to your short-term demands.

It's not that He's too busy to work you into His schedule or unconcerned with the time pressure you're up against. It's just that He knows how impatient we can get, how limited our little minds are to the bigger picture of His plan, and how often we'll look back on this season of waiting as one of the most valuable experiences our faith ever endured.

If you can ever come to grips with the fact that God knows exactly what you need, when you need it, and in what measure you need to receive it, you'll be able to lead with your chin into every thought that tempts you to begrudge His timing. After all, we've got a long time to enjoy all the things we've been waiting for.

> "What a surge of hope and adrenaline to know that because I have chosen to follow Christ, I am a victor in the only game that really matters."
>
> —Lucinda Secrest McDowell

Notes

NEXT UP *The story of the tortoise and the hare isn't found in the Bible. But it's running over with a lesson too many of us learn the hard way: Slow and steady wins the race.*

Simple Steps

Steady Progress

Not that I have already obtained all this, or have already been made perfect, but I press on to take hold of that for which Christ Jesus took hold of me. Brothers, I do not consider myself yet to have taken hold of it. But one thing I do: Forgetting what is behind and straining toward what is ahead, *I press on toward the goal to win the prize* for which God has called me heavenward in Christ Jesus.

All of us who are mature should take such a view of things. And if on some point you think differently, that too God will make clear to you. . .

Join with others in following my example, brothers, and take note of those who live according to the pattern we gave you. For, as I have often told you before and now say again even with tears, many live as enemies of the cross of Christ. Their destiny is destruction, their god is their stomach, and their glory is in their shame. Their mind is on earthly things.

But our citizenship is in heaven. And we eagerly await a Savior from there, the Lord Jesus Christ, who, by the power that enables him to bring everything under his control, will transform our lowly bodies so that they will be like his glorious body.

People who take life in quick bursts of glory miss the sustained experience of Christian victory.

Scripture
Philippians 3:12-15, 17-21

DEFINING MOMENTS

Every now and then, a football team will string together a season of surprise victories on the backs of a wide-open offense and a renegade pass rush. Fans will flock to the games, reporters will descend on their campus, front pages will flash their colors and accomplishments.

But somewhere in relative obscurity, another team will be turning their usual brand of rugged discipline, quiet confidence, and basic, fundamental football into simple, unspectacular wins. 14-10. 20-17. 10-8. Nothing all that special for the 10 o'clock highlight reel. Just another win.

> "We must be content with our daily portion, without anxious thought as to anything that may be whirling around us in God's universe."
>
> –Hannah Whitall Smith

Like expected. And five years later, when the glitter and sparkle of that Cinderella team has faded into a frustrating 5-and-6 finish, the boys who just block and tackle and run dives up the middle will be in the hunt for another championship. That's the way it is.

So don't be discouraged if your victories don't win you the chance to stand in the pulpit or get applause from the crowd. Your coach likes the way you play when you give Him consistent performance.

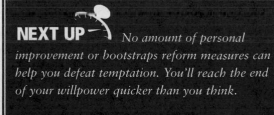

NEXT UP *No amount of personal improvement or bootstraps reform measures can help you defeat temptation. You'll reach the end of your willpower quicker than you think.*

Not on My Own

The Inadequacy of Willpower

We like to think we can will our way past the tight spots of life. We think too highly of ourselves.

For the message of the cross is foolishness to those who are perishing, but to us who are being saved it is the power of God. For it is written: "I will destroy the wisdom of the wise; the intelligence of the intelligent I will frustrate."

Where is the wise man? Where is the scholar? Where is the philosopher of this age? Has not God made foolish the wisdom of the world? . . .

For the foolishness of God is wiser than man's wisdom, and *the weakness of God is stronger than man's strength.*

Brothers, think of what you were when you were called. Not many of you were wise by human standards; not many were influential; not many were of noble birth. But God chose the foolish things of the world to shame the wise; God chose the weak things of the world to shame the strong.

He chose the lowly things of this world and the despised things—and the things that are not—to nullify the things that are, so that no one may boast before him.

It is because of him that you are in Christ Jesus, who has become for us wisdom from God—that is, our righteousness, holiness and redemption.

Scripture

1 Corinthians 1:18-20, 25-30

⚡ DEFINING MOMENTS

You can try to dodge temptation, come up with some kind of self-talk to say, or devise some clever scheme to trick your mind into thinking about something else. But in the end, all your bluster will pop like an overblown balloon and you'll find yourself right back in the mudhole.

Take it from people who've been there themselves.

Human willpower can accomplish a lot of things. But achieving lasting victory over your sin areas is not one of them.

That's why every Christian who's gotten sick enough of continuing to sin eventually throws up their hands, lays down their unwieldy weapons, and starts letting God fight their battles for them . . . "because the one who is in you is greater than the one who is in the world" (1 John 4:4).

Turn a deaf ear to temptation. Repeat the Scriptures that remind you to "count yourselves dead to sin" (Rom. 6:11) and "do not give the devil a foothold" (Eph. 4:27). "For the battle is not yours, but God's" (2 Chron. 20:15). Stay alert, sit back, and watch Him win.

> "You can't testify to your righteousness and His at the same time. You can only give witness to His righteousness in you."
>
> —Jim Gilbert

NEXT UP *It takes some truly amazing grace to turn a hardheaded, rebellious sinner into a child of the living God. But that's not the only amazing thing that grace can do.*

This Is a Hold-Up

God's Grace

You are every bit as dependent on the grace of God this minute as you were from the very start.

For the grace of God that brings salvation has appeared to all men. *It teaches us to say "No" to ungodliness and worldly passions*, and to live self-controlled, upright and godly lives in this present age, while we wait for the blessed hope—the glorious appearing of our great God and Savior, Jesus Christ, who gave himself for us to redeem us from all wickedness and to purify for himself a people that are his very own, eager to do what is good. . . .

When the kindness and love of God our Savior appeared, he saved us, not because of righteous things we had done, but because of his mercy. He saved us through the washing of rebirth and renewal by the Holy Spirit, whom he poured out on us generously through Jesus Christ our Savior, so that, having been justified by his grace, we might become heirs having the hope of eternal life.

This is a trustworthy saying. And I want you to stress these things, so that those who have trusted in God may be careful to devote themselves to doing what is good. These things are excellent and profitable for everyone. . . .

Grace be with you all.

Scripture

Titus 2:11-14; 3:4-8, 15b

♫ DEFINING MOMENTS

Every one of us knows the anguish of failing the Lord. We tap our fist against our forehead, eyes closed in disbelief and disappointment. We've done it again. How are we going to explain this to God?

But we don't have to. He already knows. And after we've beaten ourselves up long enough, we finally realize that we can quit groveling in shame and turn our face toward His throne . . . "so that we may receive mercy and find grace to help us in our time of need" (Heb. 4:16).

> "God's grace is not a suit meant for Sundays. We should wrap it around our shoulders every day of our lives."
>
> —Sheila Walsh

Grace. There it is again. Just as sweet and refreshing as it was the first time we put it to our lips. When we first fell back into its big, strong arms and felt the peace of God's purity flowing through our veins, we thought grace had done all it was supposed to do. But like ocean waves that splash with fresh blessing from a bottomless source, God's grace keeps catching us, keeps picking us up, keeps moving us forward when we thought we'd fallen too far behind to catch up. His grace is still here, still supplying, still as amazing as ever.

NEXT UP *God sees greatness in the most out-of-the-way places, where most of us pass by without a second look, but where people are doing little things of great importance.*

Unsung Heroes

Greatness in Little Things

You can never do anything too small for God. In fact, you might be surprised how big that can be.

"Again, it will be like a man going on a journey, who called his servants and entrusted his property to them. To one he gave five talents of money, to another two talents, and to another one talent, each according to his ability. Then he went on his journey.

"The man who had received the five talents went at once and put his money to work and gained five more. So also, the one with the two talents gained two more. But the man who had received the one talent went off, dug a hole in the ground and hid his master's money.

"After a long time the master of those servants returned and settled accounts with them. The man who had received the five talents brought the other five. 'Master,' he said, 'you entrusted me with five talents. See, I have gained five more.' His master replied, 'Well done, good and faithful servant! You have been faithful with a few things; I will put you in charge of many things. Come and share your master's happiness.'" . . .

"*Whoever can be trusted with very little can also be trusted with much*, and whoever is dishonest with very little will also be dishonest with much."

Scripture

Matthew 25:14-21;
Luke 16:10

꒰ DEFINING MOMENTS

Little notes written to encourage someone to keep their chin up, to remind them that God hasn't forgotten them. And neither have you.

Long, boring hours beside a hospital bed, holding the hand and whispering into the ear of a dying grandmother who may not even know you're in the room.

An hour-long, nonsensical Barbie adventure with your four-year-old (complete with your own falsetto voices) even though you were just fifty pages away from tying up the loose ends of a good mystery novel.

Great people in God's eyes are the ones who don't shun the shadows of personal ministry, but who are willing to be faithful when it doesn't show, humble when it doesn't profit, and unafraid to say no to their own self-will. "Blessed are the meek, for they will inherit the earth" (Matt. 5:5). They will know the joy of sharing a kind word, the pleasure of buying someone a cup of coffee. They will come to know quicker than the rest of us what life is all about. Life is in the little things.

> "We are expected to live triumphantly without what we would naturally wish for the most. Full provision is made for that kind of life."
>
> —Amy Carmichael

Notes

NEXT UP ⤳ *Becoming drawn to the unnoticed aspects of ministry will slowly turn the focus of your life off yourself—and into the faces and futures of those within your reach.*

Always on Call

Becoming Others-Oriented

Your will has been a tyrant all your life. It's time to start thinking about someone else for a change.

Then James and John, the sons of Zebedee, came to him. "Teacher," they said, "we want you to do for us whatever we ask."

"What do you want me to do for you?" he asked. They replied, "Let one of us sit at your right and the other at your left in your glory."

"You don't know what you are asking," Jesus said. "Can you drink the cup I drink or be baptized with the baptism I am baptized with?"

"We can," they answered. Jesus said to them, "You will drink the cup I drink and be baptized with the baptism I am baptized with, but to sit at my right or left is not for me to grant. These places belong to those for whom they have been prepared."

When the ten heard about this, they became indignant with James and John. Jesus called them together and said, "You know that those who are regarded as rulers of the Gentiles lord it over them, and their high officials exercise authority over them.

"Not so with you. Instead, whoever wants to become great among you must be your servant, and whoever wants to be first must be slave of all. *For even the Son of Man did not come to be served, but to serve*, and to give his life as a ransom for many."

Scripture

Mark 10:35-45

✎ DEFINING MOMENTS

This was supposed to be the era of the shorter work week, what with the emergence of the computer and the simpler life we'd enjoy from our modern conveniences. Our biggest challenge was supposed to be choosing how to spend all this extra time we'd have on our hands.

Very funny.

Have you ever seen a day when people were this strung out with work demands, longer hours, tighter deadlines, breakneck schedules, higher expectations? Whatever little energy is left at the end of earning a paycheck, running errands, and keeping our homes in working order usually ends up stretched out on the sofa with a glass of tea. And the hope that no one will bother us. At this pace, we just don't have time for people.

> "As we give ourselves to God, He gives back to us a wonderful present—the power to demonstrate Christ's love to those He sends our way."
>
> —Doris Greig

What an opportunity, then, for you to make the love of Christ stand out in a crowd—every time you forsake the sofa in order to meet a need, serve a brother, help a neighbor. The window's open for us to "shine like stars in the universe" (Phil. 2:15). And see God's face light up.

NEXT UP ✎ *The table is set for you to be a chosen tool in the hand of God, to be the lens that people look through to feel His love, experience His grace—and to find His life.*

A Life of Service

Devoted to Ministry

> The happiest you will ever be is when you're giving of yourself to others. Try it and see.

His divine power has given us everything we need for life and godliness through our knowledge of him who called us by his own glory and goodness. Through these he has given us his very great and precious promises, so that through them you may participate in the divine nature and escape the corruption in the world caused by evil desires.

For this very reason, make every effort to add to your faith goodness; and to goodness, knowledge; and to knowledge, self-control; and to self-control, perseverance; and to perseverance, godliness; and to godliness, brotherly kindness; and to brotherly kindness, love.

For if you possess these qualities in increasing measure, they will keep you from being ineffective and unproductive in your knowledge of our Lord Jesus Christ. But if anyone does not have them, he is nearsighted and blind, and has forgotten that he has been cleansed from his past sins.

Therefore, my brothers, be all the more eager to make your calling and election sure. For if you do these things, you will never fall, and you will receive a rich welcome into the eternal kingdom of our Lord and Savior Jesus Christ.

Scripture

2 Peter 1:3-11

Notes

〰 DEFINING MOMENTS

He was 88 years old. Old enough to know what he was talking about. And you just happened to catch him on a day when he really felt like talking. You had gone with your church group to a local nursing home—sort of a ministry project. You weren't all that sure about it at first; but, as often happens when you try something new like that, God puts just the right people in your path. And yours was a talker.

Because you are a polite person, you tried hard not to interrupt or to let on that people were waiting for you. Some of his ramblings were hard to follow, but you nodded a lot, acting genuinely interested.

Then he leaned forward in his chair, raised his crooked finger to your face, squinted his eyes through thick, heavy glasses, as though he saw in you every precious moment of life he wished he could recapture, and said: "I want you to listen to this old man: Love people. Do good to people. Go out of your way to help people. People are all that matter."

Take it from a guy who knows. People are all that matter.

> "Jesus is the leader. I am the follower. My goal today is to follow His schedule, accomplish His agenda, and love whoever He sends my way."
>
> —John Kramp

NEXT UP → *Along with a new mindset comes a new set of Christian characteristics that are yours to develop, yours to enjoy, and yours to use as proof that this God of yours is real.*

SECTION 5

Sure Signs of Growth

Wearing the name of Christian can draw a lot of fire from
other people—those who'd rather blame the world's
problems on church hypocrisy than to deal squarely with
their own lives. But you'll rarely convince them of God's
love with clever words and persuasion. You'll win them
over by bearing fruit that tastes too good to resist.

All Is Well

Peace

Knowing that Jesus Christ is in charge can put you at ease in life's most unsettling situations.

Therefore, since we have been justified through faith, we have peace with God through our Lord Jesus Christ, through whom we have gained access by faith into this grace in which we now stand. And we rejoice in the hope of the glory of God. . . .

Rejoice in the Lord always. I will say it again: Rejoice! Let your gentleness be evident to all. The Lord is near. Do not be anxious about anything, but in everything, by prayer and petition, with thanksgiving, present your requests to God. And the peace of God, which transcends all understanding, will guard your hearts and your minds in Christ Jesus. . . .

Many are asking, "Who can show us any good?" Let the light of your face shine upon us, O Lord.

You have filled my heart with greater joy than when their grain and new wine abound.

I will lie down and sleep in peace, for you alone, O Lord, make me dwell in safety. . . .

You will keep in perfect peace him whose mind is steadfast, because he trusts in you.

Trust in the Lord forever, for the Lord, the Lord, is the Rock eternal.

Scripture

Romans 5:1-2; Philippians 4:4-7; Psalm 4:6-8; Isaiah 26:3-4

DEFINING MOMENTS

Train wrecks don't appear all that often on the evening news. But if you'll look around you, in the lives of people you know (or at least people you know of), you'll see one just about every day.

That's because life can roll on fairly predictably for a long time, seducing its passengers into laying their heads back on their own self-assurance. But sooner or later, they'll encounter some kind of unexpected turbulence—a phone call at four in the morning, a chest pain that keeps flaring up, a teenage son who's shutting them out of his world—the frightening feeling that life is no longer in the safekeeping of cruise control.

That's when people long for peace: when in the panic of life's emergencies, help seems a million miles away—when in the lonely hours of the night, they wish they had a friend like God to talk to . . . the way you do.

You are a witness of God's peace every time you keep a cool head through one of life's hot spots. Be on your guard. Your trust is showing.

> Notes

> "A mark of spiritual maturity is the quiet confidence that God is in control—without the need to understand why He does what He does."
>
> —Charles Swindoll

NEXT UP *You're not going to get everything you want out of life. But God has promised to make sure you get everything you need. And you can learn to be content with that.*

I Am Satisfied

Contentment

How much time and energy could you save if you were just happy with what you already have?

I know what it is to be in need, and I know what it is to have plenty. *I have learned the secret of being content in any and every situation,* whether well fed or hungry, whether living in plenty or in want. I can do everything through him who gives me strength. . . .

If anyone teaches false doctrines and does not agree to the sound instruction of our Lord Jesus Christ and to godly teaching, he is conceited and understands nothing.

He has an unhealthy interest in controversies and quarrels about words that result in envy, strife, malicious talk, evil suspicions and constant friction between men of corrupt mind, who have been robbed of the truth and who think that godliness is a means to financial gain.

But godliness with contentment is great gain. For we brought nothing into the world, and we can take nothing out of it. But if we have food and clothing, we will be content with that.

People who want to get rich fall into temptation and a trap and into many foolish and harmful desires that plunge men into ruin and destruction. For the love of money is a root of all kinds of evil.

Scripture

Philippians 4:12-13;
1 Timothy 6:3-10

⚡ DEFINING MOMENTS

Christian contentment goes a lot deeper than the cars in our driveway or the clothes in our closet. In fact, it doesn't usually take long for us to understand—in our head, if not entirely in practice—that we can be OK with the things we've got, even if they're not the latest, the fastest, the sharpest. We learn quickly that we can't really keep pace in that game. Today's prize trophy ends up in tomorrow's garage sale.

But contentment is much more than a material matter. It's about waking up in the morning satisfied with who we are—not with what sin has done to us, but with what God has invested in us. It means being content with our basic temperament and the role God uses us to play in life. Content with the work He has given us, even if at the time it seems an improper match with the calling we feel. Content with being a person of honor and integrity, even if it seems like people are laughing at us.

You can stop searching now. In Jesus Christ, you have found life's ultimate fulfillment. Be at peace with the person He's helping you to be.

Notes

> "Contentment is a learned behavior, an acquired skill. It doesn't just happen when you fall into the right set of circumstances."
>
> —Mary Hunt

NEXT UP ✍ *Humble people don't tend to attract a lot of attention, not because they feel unworthy, but because they know the value of serving people where only God can see it.*

Don't Thank Me

Humility

Want to feel good about yourself when you lie down at night? Think about others through the day.

With what shall I come before the Lord and bow down before the exalted God? Shall I come before him with burnt offerings, with calves a year old?

Will the Lord be pleased with thousands of rams, with ten thousand rivers of oil? Shall I offer my first-born for my transgression, the fruit of my body for the sin of my soul?

He has showed you, O man, what is good. And what does the Lord require of you? To act justly and to love mercy and to walk humbly with your God. . . .

Do not withhold good from those who deserve it, when it is in your power to act. Do not say to your neighbor, "Come back later; I'll give it tomorrow"— when you now have it with you. . . .

Finally, all of you, live in harmony with one another; be sympathetic, love as brothers, be compassionate and humble. . . .

Clothe yourselves with humility toward one another, because, *"God opposes the proud but gives grace to the humble."*

Humble yourselves, therefore, under God's mighty hand, that he may lift you up in due time.

Scripture

Micah 6:6-8; Proverbs 3:27-28; 1 Peter 3:8; 5:5b-6

✒ DEFINING MOMENTS

You wouldn't know him. He lived in a small town and preached in a small church, earning a salary so small that he had to take a job at a local clothing factory to provide for his wife and family. Even in stature he was small, not the kind of man who entered a room with an immediate presence. You could have passed him in the mall or waited behind him in line at the grocery store and not have paid him much attention.

But this small man with the small life was a giant among men, backing up his Sunday morning words with a long, unassuming list of all-week-long actions. Who knows how many times his neighbors had seen him at their door with a sackful of beans and tomatoes from his garden or how many times an elderly widow had heard his mower starting up in her yard? Or how many strangers had literally received the shirt (and probably even the coat) right off his back?

You wouldn't know. He'd never say.

It takes big people to be truly humble.

> "Learn to be unknown. To think of oneself as nothing, and to think well and highly of others is the best and most perfect wisdom."
>
> —Thomas á Kempis

NEXT UP *If peace is God's answer to panic, if contentment is His answer to greed, if humility is His answer to personal recognition, what's His answer to worry? Be patient.*

Notes

Waiting Your Turn

Patience

The light will eventually turn green for you. And you'll understand why you needed to wait so long.

Be patient, then, brothers, until the Lord's coming. See how the farmer waits for the land to yield its valuable crop and how patient he is for the autumn and spring rains. You too, be patient and stand firm, because the Lord's coming is near. Don't grumble against each other, brothers, or you will be judged. The Judge is standing at the door!

Brothers, as an example of patience in the face of suffering, take the prophets who spoke in the name of the Lord. As you know, we consider blessed those who have persevered. You have heard of Job's perseverance and have seen what the Lord finally brought about. The Lord is full of compassion and mercy. . . .

To you, O Lord, I lift up my soul; in you I trust, O my God. . . .

No one whose hope is in you will ever be put to shame, but they will be put to shame who are treacherous without excuse.

Show me your ways, O Lord, teach me your paths; guide me in your truth and teach me, for *you are God my Savior, and my hope is in you all day long.*

Remember, O Lord, your great mercy and love, for they are from of old.

Scripture
James 5:7-11; Psalm 25:1, 3-6

⅃ꜱ **DEFINING MOMENTS**

Monday. "God, I believe this is the week I'm going to hear about that job. I'm going to be patient, though. I know you're in control."

Tuesday. "God, I was really hoping to hear something yesterday, but that's OK. I just need you to help me be patient till I hear."

Wednesday. "I've just got to hear something one way or the other—but I don't want to sound desperate to them or anything. Maybe I should just wait. But they might think I'm not really interested if I don't check back with them. I don't know what to do. God, what do I do? I can't wait any longer."

Thursday. "I can't believe it. They must be going with somebody else. God, I don't understand. I mean, here it is, 7 o'clock on Thursday night, and I still don't—"

"Hello? Oh, that's OK. I got the job? Really? Sure, Monday sounds fine. OK, well, I'll talk to you then. OK, thanks!"

"Wow! I got the job. I got the job! I can't believe it! I can't—I can't believe how impatient I was with you, God. I'll learn, won't I?"

> "God uses the time while we are waiting for His promises to be fulfilled to make us ready for the answer."
>
> —Neva Coyle

NEXT UP *Anybody can smile big. But the only people who can be happy down where it counts—in any situation—are those who've made Jesus Christ the joy of their lives.*

Better Than Ever

Joy

There's something that only Christ can give you that's a whole lot better than happiness. Enjoy!

I will exalt you, O Lord, for you lifted me out of the depths and did not let my enemies gloat over me.

O Lord my God, I called to you for help and you healed me. O Lord, you brought me up from the grave; you spared me from going down into the pit.

Sing to the Lord, you saints of his; praise his holy name. For his anger lasts only a moment, but his favor lasts a lifetime; *weeping may remain for a night, but rejoicing comes in the morning.*

When I felt secure, I said, "I shall never be shaken." O Lord, when you favored me, you made my mountain stand firm; but when you hid your face, I was dismayed.

To you, O Lord, I called; to the Lord I cried for mercy: "What gain is there in my destruction, in my going down into the pit? Will the dust praise you? Will it proclaim your faithfulness? Hear, O Lord, and be merciful to me; O Lord, be my help."

You turned my wailing into dancing; you removed my sackcloth and clothed me with joy, that my heart may sing to you and not be silent. O Lord my God, I will give you thanks forever.

Scripture

Psalm 30:1-12

⤳ DEFINING MOMENTS

You've seen people who had joy. They're the ones who know how to throw their head back and belly-laugh at a good, clean joke. They're the ones who get as much pleasure out of a bowl of vanilla ice cream and chocolate syrup as most people require from a steak and lobster dinner. They're the ones who still cry every time Travis has to shoot Ole Yeller and wonder why they can't make movies like they used to.

That's because joy is so full, so rich, so big-hearted, it can't be contained in a smile. The joy that God gives to those whose sins are forgiven, whose destiny is certain, and whose hearts beat for other people pours out through all their emotions—and showers the brightness of God's presence into scenes and situations that seem as dark as death.

"The joy of the Lord is your strength" (Neh. 8:10). And as you grow deeper in His Word, more enthralled with His love, ever nearer to His side, He'll show you reasons to be glad everywhere you turn. And chances to share the exuberance with everyone you meet.

> "Wherever you are, be all there. Live to the hilt every situation you believe to be the will of God."
>
> —Jim Elliot

NEXT UP *While you're building your spiritual muscles on the freeweights of joy, you're likely to meet another virtue that can strip away unneeded inches of the flesh.*

Keep It Basic

Simplicity

It's not easy to do, but it's actually very simple: Put God first, and the rest will take care of itself.

> *Make it your ambition to lead a quiet life,* to mind your own business and to work with your hands, just as we told you, so that your daily life may win the respect of outsiders and so that you will not be dependent on anybody. . . .

Therefore each of you must put off falsehood and speak truthfully to his neighbor, for we are all members of one body. "In your anger do not sin": Do not let the sun go down while you are still angry, and do not give the devil a foothold. He who has been stealing must steal no longer, but must work, doing something useful with his own hands, that he may have something to share with those in need.

Do not let any unwholesome talk come out of your mouths, but only what is helpful for building others up according to their needs, that it may benefit those who listen. And do not grieve the Holy Spirit of God, with whom you were sealed for the day of redemption. Get rid of all bitterness, rage and anger, brawling and slander, along with every form of malice. Be kind and compassionate to one another, forgiving each other, just as in Christ God forgave you.

Scripture

1 Thessalonians 4:11-12;
Ephesians 4:25-32

Notes

✑ DEFINING MOMENTS

"I just wish I could simplify my life."

If you've said it once, you've said it a hundred times—and watched every head in the room nod in personal agreement. This modern world with its maxed-out credit cards and multi-year car notes, with its ten-hour days and ten-errand nights, has stripped the threads on our ability to cope and left us spinning our wheels just to stay above water.

But God has your answer. It's not a week at the beach or a thousand dollars in the mail from a rich uncle. It's a singleminded purpose to love and serve Him through every circumstance in your life.

> "Holy simplicity is a life that has become simple in its integrity, devotion, and inner freedom, a life that simply belongs to God alone."
>
> —James Houston

Imagine waking up in the morning with the exact same demands and pressures, but with a real confidence that God was going to use every one of them to make your life more useful to Him, to put you in the path of people who need your touch, to give you new understanding and insights that are secretly preparing you for the next big challenge you'll face. When God has your heart, He can help you handle all your headaches.

NEXT UP *Even your physical body has received a new touch from God through your salvation experience with Christ. And you have a responsibility to keep it clean.*

Tending the Temple

Self-Control

You may not be all that crazy about the body God gave you. But it's His house now. Don't junk it up.

"Everything is permissible for me"—but not everything is beneficial. "Everything is permissible for me"—but I will not be mastered by anything.

"Food for the stomach and the stomach for food"—but God will destroy them both. The body is not meant for sexual immorality, but for the Lord, and the Lord for the body.

By his power God raised the Lord from the dead, and he will raise us also.

Do you not know that your bodies are members of Christ himself? Shall I then take the members of Christ and unite them with a prostitute? Never!

Do you not know that he who unites himself with a prostitute is one with her in body? For it is said, "The two will become one flesh." But he who unites himself with the Lord is one with him in spirit.

Flee from sexual immorality. All other sins a man commits are outside his body, but he who sins sexually sins against his own body.

Do you not know that your body is a temple of the Holy Spirit, who is in you, whom you have received from God? You are not your own; you were bought at a price. Therefore honor God with your body.

Scripture

1 Corinthians 6:12-20

⤷ DEFINING MOMENTS

There's something sacred about God's house. That's why you wouldn't feel good eating a Whopper Junior during church. Or wiping your muddy shoes on the pew cushions. Or telling a dirty joke from the pulpit. You just don't do those things in the church building. You have too much respect for it, if not for your own personal reputation. Even the Christmas and Easter crowd knows that.

> "We were purchased out of the slavemarket of sin by Jesus Christ Himself. We have no right to injure property that doesn't belong to us."
>
> —O. S. Hawkins

But guess what. Those two eyes you're peeping out of right now are windows to the house of God. Those two ears on your head are its sound system. And everything your hands choose to do, everywhere your feet choose to go, is visible on the screen of your heart. In the sanctuary of your soul. In the living, breathing temple of the one true God. In you.

So when you're always picking candy bars over carrot sticks, when you're constantly choosing the TV over the treadmill—and when you're giving in to sexual temptation instead of walking the path of purity—you're doing it right in God's living room. Don't you ever forget it.

NEXT UP *You've already believed the unbelievable—that the God of heaven loves you with an everlasting love. So why is it so hard to believe that He can do whatever He says?*

I Still Believe

Faith

When your eyes can't see it, it's hard to believe it. But nothing in this world is impossible with God.

When Jesus had finished saying all this in the hearing of the people, he entered Capernaum. There a centurion's servant, whom his master valued highly, was sick and about to die. The centurion heard of Jesus and sent some elders of the Jews to him, asking him to come and heal his servant. When they came to Jesus, they pleaded earnestly with him, "This man deserves to have you do this, because he loves our nation and has built our synagogue." So Jesus went with them.

He was not far from the house when the centurion sent friends to say to him: "Lord, don't trouble yourself, for I do not deserve to have you come under my roof. That is why I did not even consider myself worthy to come to you. But say the word, and my servant will be healed. For I myself am a man under authority, with soldiers under me. I tell this one, 'Go,' and he goes; and that one, 'Come,' and he comes. I say to my servant, 'Do this,' and he does it."

When Jesus heard this, he was amazed at him, and turning to the crowd following him, he said, *"I tell you, I have not found such great faith even in Israel."* Then the men who had been sent returned to the house and found the servant well.

Scripture

Luke 7:1-10

DEFINING MOMENTS

Worst-case scenario. You've been diagnosed with a life-threatening illness. It's not a very aggressive one, but the doctors say that slowly—over time—even the most routine, ordinary activities of life will become taxing and laborious. The outlook doesn't look good.

But you go to God. And you pray with all the faith you can muster. You honestly believe that He's going to heal you. You really do.

Over the years, however, your prognosis plays out pretty much according to schedule. Yet your faith never wavers. In fact, you wish you had a dime for every time God's given you some little reason to hope—almost always at the moment that anger or depression was coming close to claiming you.

> "A person of faith may experience loss but not emptiness, disappointment but not despair, adversity but not defeat."
>
> —Dorothy Kelley Patterson

As your strength fails, your friends and family rally around to serve you. You stay upbeat, believing, being as much of a blessing to them as they are to you. You live a life free from the petty worries of the every-day person. And though you die too soon, you leave behind a legacy of faith—a faith that accomplished more than you'll ever know.

NEXT UP *One of the trademark traits of the Christian life is the ability to be truly thankful—thankful to God, thankful to others, thankful for everything that comes your way.*

Thanks for Everything

Gratitude

Going out of your way to thank someone will go a long way toward growing your character.

Now on his way to Jerusalem, Jesus traveled along the border between Samaria and Galilee. As he was going into a village, ten men who had leprosy met him. They stood at a distance and called out in a loud voice, "Jesus, Master, have pity on us!"

When he saw them, he said, "Go, show yourselves to the priests." And as they went, they were cleansed.

One of them, when he saw he was healed, came back, praising God in a loud voice. He threw himself at Jesus' feet and thanked him—and he was a Samaritan.

Jesus asked, "Were not all ten cleansed? Where are the other nine? Was no one found to return and give praise to God except this foreigner?" Then he said to him, "Rise and go; your faith has made you well. . . ."

Let the peace of Christ rule in your hearts, since as members of one body you were called to peace. *And be thankful*. Let the word of Christ dwell in you richly as you teach and admonish one another with all wisdom, and as you sing psalms, hymns and spiritual songs with gratitude in your hearts to God. And whatever you do, whether in word or deed, do it all in the name of the Lord Jesus, giving thanks to God the Father through him.

Scripture

Luke 17:11-19;
Colossians 3:15-17

DEFINING MOMENTS

Yes, we live in a world where waiters can sometimes be slow getting us more coffee, where repairmen can only promise they'll be at our house sometime between eight and five, where computer terminals can mysteriously go down the moment we call needing important information.

That's life.

But, my, how this world needs a lot more thankfulness. People who can smile back into the face of a harried store worker and thank her for at least trying. People who are more willing to write a note of appreciation than to register a hotheaded complaint. People who don't forget the ones who gave them a chance when no one else gave them the time of day. People who work just as hard for five dollars an hour as they would for ten.

> "Our receiving of things isn't dependent on our giving thanks, but oh—how it pleases God when we simply look up and say, Thank you."
> —Gigi Graham Tchividijan

If you want to make an impact for Christ on ordinary people in your world, just try being genuinely thankful for even the smallest kindnesses done to you. And it won't be long before they recognize you as a person who walks with God because you treat them like someone special.

NEXT UP *Put all the qualities of the Christian life into one nice package; pile them up as high as you like. But make sure they're wrapped in only one ribbon—the ribbon of love.*

The Greatest of These

Love

Dear friends, let us love one another, for love comes from God. Everyone who loves has been born of God and knows God. Whoever does not love does not know God, because God is love.

This is how God showed his love among us: He sent his one and only Son into the world that we might live through him.

This is love: not that we loved God, but that he loved us and sent his Son as an atoning sacrifice for our sins.

Dear friends, *since God so loved us, we also ought to love one another.* . . .

In this way, love is made complete among us so that we will have confidence on the day of judgment, because in this world we are like him.

There is no fear in love. But perfect love drives out fear, because fear has to do with punishment. The one who fears is not made perfect in love.

We love because he first loved us. If anyone says, "I love God," yet hates his brother, he is a liar. For anyone who does not love his brother, whom he has seen, cannot love God, whom he has not seen. And he has given us this command: Whoever loves God must also love his brother.

Scripture

1 John 4:7-11, 17-21

Life can get you into some difficult situations. But love can get you through anything.

✒ DEFINING MOMENTS

New Bible translations have certainly succeeded in bringing the Scriptures within everyday reach. And that's great. But sometimes in the course of communicating, they must sacrifice beauty for practicality, giving us the command (for example) to "love each other deeply," when the old King James Version puts it so eloquently: "Above all things have fervent charity among yourselves" (1 Pet. 4:8).

> "To truly love someone means that we will always place that person's welfare above our own. This, after all, is how God loves us."
>
> –Carol Fitzpatrick

Fervent isn't a word you'd usually place alongside love (or charity, to toss out another old-time term). You might describe a Crossfire argument as fervent. Or the guy who paints his face in the team colors.

But how about helping a friend move on the first Saturday you've had off this month? How about organizing two weeks of meals for the family whose newborn baby is still too sick to leave the hospital? How about replacing a water pump for free on your Sunday School teacher's car?

When your love for one another is fervent, it's thought-out, planned, and deliberate. It's a love that meets each other's needs. With a passion.

NEXT UP ✏ *But just as diligently as you're feeding your spirit with the rare qualities of the Christian life, it's important to feed your mind with the truths of the Christian faith.*

SECTION

Nice Things to Know

If all you have to go on is your own experience, you
don't have much more to say about your faith than anyone
who claims to believe anything. But when your words are
based on the timeless Word of God, you have a real leg to
stand on. And a legacy of faithful men and women who've
built their lives on the same foundation.

Faith Over Feelings

Sound Doctrine

The first step in understanding what Christians believe is to just let the Bible speak for itself.

But as for you, *continue in what you have learned and have become convinced of,* because you know those from whom you learned it, and how from infancy you have known the holy Scriptures, which are able to make you wise for salvation through faith in Christ Jesus.

All Scripture is God-breathed and is useful for teaching, rebuking, correcting and training in righteousness, so that the man of God may be thoroughly equipped for every good work.

In the presence of God and of Christ Jesus, who will judge the living and the dead, and in view of his appearing and his kingdom, I give you this charge: Preach the Word; be prepared in season and out of season; correct, rebuke and encourage—with great patience and careful instruction.

For the time will come when men will not put up with sound doctrine. Instead, to suit their own desires, they will gather around them a great number of teachers to say what their itching ears want to hear. They will turn their ears away from the truth and turn aside to myths.

But you, keep your head in all situations, endure hardship, do the work of an evangelist, discharge all the duties of your ministry.

Scripture
2 Timothy 3:14-4:5

DEFINING MOMENTS

To have nothing more than head knowledge about Jesus Christ is certainly inadequate to understand who He really is. But to have nothing more than heart knowledge is just about as dangerous . . . because if all you know is what you feel, you may later feel differently about what you think you know.

"The heart is deceitful above all things and beyond cure. Who can understand it?" (Jer. 17:9). Why should you trust in your own observations and experiences, when God has given you written reasons for everything He is and everything you are—right out there where you can see it, read it, examine it, study it, and picture the whole thing in even more vivid detail than you've seen with your own eyes?

Doctrine sounds so highbrow and sophisticated. But if this faith of yours is as important as you say, don't you want to know all you can about it? Don't you want to be able to answer others' questions with confidence in the facts? Don't you want to have His Word to hold on to?

> "We need theology, not to replace experience, but to give it definition and to ensure its spiritual health."
>
> —Dan Scott

NEXT UP ☞ *We may think a new singing group is awesome. We may think water skiing is awesome. We may think three-cheese nachos are awesome. No—God is awesome.*

Notes

Bigger than Life

God's Holiness

> He's our Father. He's our Friend. But this God of ours is holy. And we do well to remember it.

 The Lord reigns, let the earth be glad; let the distant shores rejoice.

Clouds and thick darkness surround him; righteousness and justice are the foundation of his throne.

Fire goes before him and consumes his foes on every side. His lightning lights up the world; the earth sees and trembles.

The mountains melt like wax before the Lord, before the Lord of all the earth.

The heavens proclaim his righteousness, and all the peoples see his glory.

All who worship images are put to shame, those who boast in idols—worship him, all you gods!

Zion hears and rejoices and the villages of Judah are glad because of your judgments, O Lord.

For you, O Lord, are the Most High over all the earth; you are exalted far above all gods.

Let those who love the Lord hate evil, for he guards the lives of his faithful ones and delivers them from the hand of the wicked.

Light is shed upon the righteous and joy on the upright in heart.

Rejoice in the Lord, you who are righteous, and praise his holy name.

Scripture

Psalm 97:1-12

Notes

⌇ DEFINING MOMENTS

In trying to make God appetizing to a wide range of tastes, some of us have been guilty of making Him a little too warm and fuzzy. In trying to keep His high standards from coming across as too gruff or unsettling, we've been tempted to soften His message and let people find out the rest once they've already committed.

We've been trying to be God's PR people.

But even though the Bible shows us a God whose love defines the true meaning of caring and compassion, it also tells us to "Worship the Lord in the splendor of his holiness; tremble before him, all the earth" (Ps. 96:9). His grace means nothing if it's not pictured against His perfection, and His mercy loses its luster if it's not framed in His justice.

God wants you close. He's sent His Son to pave the way. But it's only as you bow before Him in humility and reverent fear, staring into the pure whiteness of His glorious face, that you can realize how much He must love you—how much you love Him.

> "We place ourselves in great peril if we seek to render God as a plaything of our piety, an ornamental decoration on the religious life."
>
> —David Wells

NEXT UP *This holy God, who could have squished us all like a bug and started over from scratch if He'd wanted to, has no greater desire than to have fellowship with us.*

Priority 1

God's Plan of Redemption

Everything God does is for one single purpose: to make people see just how much He loves them.

For Christ's love compels us, because we are convinced that one died for all, and therefore all died. And he died for all, that those who live should no longer live for themselves but for him who died for them and was raised again.

So from now on we regard no one from a worldly point of view. Though we once regarded Christ in this way, we do so no longer. Therefore, if anyone is in Christ, he is a new creation; the old has gone, the new has come! All this is from *God, who reconciled us to himself through Christ* and gave us the ministry of reconciliation: that God was reconciling the world to himself in Christ, not counting men's sins against them. And he has committed to us the message of reconciliation.

We are therefore Christ's ambassadors, as though God were making his appeal through us. We implore you on Christ's behalf: Be reconciled to God.

God made him who had no sin to be sin for us, so that in him we might become the righteousness of God.

As God's fellow workers we urge you not to receive God's grace in vain. For he says, "In the time of my favor I heard you, and in the day of salvation I helped you." I tell you, now is the time of God's favor, now is the day of salvation.

Scripture

2 Corinthians 5:14-6:2

꒰ **DEFINING MOMENTS**

God could have wrapped this thing up years ago. He holds the keys in His hands right now that could turn the lights out on our perceived reality any second He wanted, then replace it with His own eternal reality. Just that quick. Just that easy.

But that's just not His way.

"The Lord is not slow in keeping his promise, as some understand slowness. He is patient with you, not wanting anyone to perish, but everyone to come to repentance" (2 Pet. 3:9).

> "God's primary goal for a person in this life is that he or she comes to know Him in a personal way."
> —Henry Blackaby

If God had His way, the devil would spend all eternity in his wicked little hell-world all by himself, with just the rats and alligators to keep him torturous company. God's passionate desire is that every person He created would appeal his self-imposed death sentence and embrace the full, free pardon that's offered through the blood of Jesus Christ.

But not forcing His way onto anyone, He patiently waits. Extending His hand. Offering the only way home. Strongly desiring His people to take it.

NEXT UP *The Way came by way of a manger in Bethlehem, where we witnessed the most incredible love story of all time: the God of heaven bending low to save the sons of earth.*

God With Us

The Incarnation

> Nothing prepared the world for seeing God in such a personal way . . . except its need for a Savior.

Nevertheless, there will be no more gloom for those who were in distress. In the past he humbled the land of Zebulun and the land of Naphtali, but in the future he will honor Galilee of the Gentiles, by the way of the sea, along the Jordan—

The people walking in darkness have seen a great light; on those living in the land of the shadow of death a light has dawned.

You have enlarged the nation and increased their joy; they rejoice before you as people rejoice at the harvest, as men rejoice when dividing the plunder.

For as in the day of Midian's defeat, you have shattered the yoke that burdens them, the bar across their shoulders, the rod of their oppressor. Every warrior's boot used in battle and every garment rolled in blood will be destined for burning, will be fuel for the fire.

For to us a child is born, to us a son is given, and the government will be on his shoulders. And he will be called Wonderful Counselor, Mighty God, Everlasting Father, Prince of Peace.

Of the increase of his government and peace there will be no end. He will reign on David's throne and over his kingdom, establishing and upholding it with justice and righteousness from that time on and for ever.

Scripture

Isaiah 9:1-7

ᥩ **DEFINING MOMENTS**

The first-century Jews may have been anticipating the coming of their Messiah with about the same low-level assurance we feel that He's coming back this afternoon. We know it's possible. We don't see how things could get much worse. But too few of us are expecting Him to be here before we go bed tonight. I mean, people have been talking about it for years. What makes us so sure that ours is the chosen generation?

But we have a pretty good idea of what it will look like when He does come. "For the Lord himself will come down from heaven, with a loud command, with the voice of the archangel and with the trumpet call of God" (1 Thess. 4:16). We know what we're looking for—just like they did. They were looking for a deliverer. A warrior king like their beloved David, who would rally God's people together and throw off the weight of Roman domination and years of oppression at the hands of their enemies.

Who'd have thought to look for their warrior in the nursery?

> "Christ, when you were in the womb of your mother, you married yourself to our mortality, that we would not remain mortal forever."
>
> —Augustine

NEXT UP *Do you realize what Christ's coming did for you? Do you understand how clean you are from the stain of sin? Do you know what God sees when He looks at you?*

Clean Slate

Justification

As for you, you were dead in your transgressions and sins, in which you used to live when you followed the ways of this world and of the ruler of the kingdom of the air, the spirit who is now at work in those who are disobedient.

All of us also lived among them at one time, gratifying the cravings of our sinful nature and following its desires and thoughts. Like the rest, we were by nature objects of wrath.

But because of his great love for us, God, who is rich in mercy, made us alive with Christ even when we were dead in transgressions—it is by grace you have been saved.

And God raised us up with Christ and seated us with him in the heavenly realms in Christ Jesus, in order that in the coming ages he might show the incomparable riches of his grace, expressed in his kindness to us in Christ Jesus.

For it is by grace you have been saved, through faith—and this not from yourselves, it is the gift of God—not by works, so that no one can boast.

For we are God's workmanship, created in Christ Jesus to do good works, which God prepared in advance for us to do.

There's a book in God's library that lists all the sins He's holding against you. Your page is blank.

Scripture

Ephesians 2:1-10

⤴ DEFINING MOMENTS

The fact that you deal with your own sins every day can often cloud the fact that God dealt with them two thousand years ago—all of them—the sins you committed two years ago, the sins you'll commit two years from now, the sins you're trying really hard not to commit today. No matter how your sins stack up on the timeline of your life, every one of them was in the future tense when Christ was gasping for air on the cross, blood oozing from His hands, His head, His feet, His side. When you gave in to His love and welcomed His forgiveness into your life, He "canceled the written code, with its regulations, that was against us and that stood opposed to us; he took it away, nailing it to the cross" (Col. 2:14). "Since we have now been justified by his blood, how much more shall we be saved from God's wrath through him!" (Rom. 5:9).

Justified. The books balanced. The debt paid. So that when God looks at you, he sees you "holy in his sight, without blemish and free from accusation" (Col. 1:22). You can't get any cleaner than that.

> "Let it be accounted folly, frenzy, fury, or whatever. We care for no knowledge in the world but this: that man hath sinned and God hath suffered."
>
> —Richard Hooker

NEXT UP *You painted a beautiful, living picture of this eternal reality the moment you slipped under the waters of baptism . . . and washed your sins into oblivion.*

Notes

Picture Perfect

Baptism

Even though different churches handle it different ways, baptism unites us with the family of God.

For Christ died for sins once for all, the righteous for the unrighteous, to bring you to God. He was put to death in the body but made alive by the Spirit, through whom also he went and preached to the spirits in prison who disobeyed long ago when God waited patiently in the days of Noah while the ark was being built. In it only a few people, eight in all, were saved through water, and this water symbolizes baptism that now saves you also—not the removal of dirt from the body but the pledge of a good conscience toward God. . . .

You are all sons of God through faith in Christ Jesus, for all of *you who were baptized into Christ have clothed yourselves with Christ.* There is neither Jew nor Greek, slave nor free, male nor female, for you are all one in Christ Jesus. . . .

In him you were also circumcised, in the putting off of the sinful nature, not with a circumcision done by the hands of men but with the circumcision done by Christ, having been buried with him in baptism and raised with him through your faith in the power of God, who raised him from the dead.

Scripture
1 Peter 3:18-21; Galatians 3:26-28; Colossians 2:11-12

✍ DEFINING MOMENTS

We could sit here and argue about whether you should be sprinkled or dunked, or about whether baptism is the moment of salvation. People who are a lot smarter than any of us have gone back and forth on these issues for centuries and are still not agreed on all the particulars. But let's not allow the incidentals to obscure the importance of this obedient act and the value it holds in the life of every Christian believer.

Could there be a more perfect, wordless way to describe what Christ has done for us or to demonstrate what has happened in our own lives by surrendering to His grace?

He died and was buried. But He rose again, conquering the finality of death. Our old selves, destined for hell and all its torments, have been buried, but raised dripping wet in the cleansing blood of Jesus Christ to walk a clear path to glory.

If you haven't yet followed Christ's example of baptism, you really should. If you already have, use its memory to remind the devil of the day you shook the sin off your feet and turned your back on him forever.

Notes

> "We are united to Jesus and to one another. We died His death and have been raised in His resurrection. Now we can follow Him."
>
> —Larry Richards

NEXT UP *When Jesus rose from the grave and ascended back home into the heavens, He took His seat at the right hand of God's throne. And He took on Himself a new job.*

A Friend in High Places

Christ, Our High Priest

Now there have been many of those priests, since death prevented them from continuing in office; but because Jesus lives forever, he has a permanent priesthood. Therefore he is able to save completely those who come to God through him, because he always lives to intercede for them.

Such a high priest meets our need—one who is holy, blameless, pure, set apart from sinners, exalted above the heavens.

Unlike the other high priests, he does not need to offer sacrifices day after day, first for his own sins, and then for the sins of the people. *He sacrificed for their sins once for all when he offered himself....*

Therefore, brothers, since we have confidence to enter the Most Holy Place by the blood of Jesus, by a new and living way opened for us through the curtain, that is, his body, and since we have a great priest over the house of God, let us draw near to God with a sincere heart in full assurance of faith, having our hearts sprinkled to cleanse us from a guilty conscience and having our bodies washed with pure water.

Let us hold unswervingly to the hope we profess, for he who promised is faithful.

Even in your quiet time, you're not really alone. Jesus is there to pray even harder than you do.

Scripture

Hebrews 7:23-27; 10:19-23

DEFINING MOMENTS

Three of the gospels report it. It must have been something to see. The moment the last breath drained out of Jesus' body, "the curtain of the temple was torn in two from top to bottom" (Matt. 27:51). For the first time ever, people could turn and see behind the thick, heavily embroidered veil that hid the deep, candle-lit darkness of God's presence—the Holy of Holies. Suddenly the sacred sanctuary which only the high priest could enter—and even at that, only once a year—was made available to the most common of men. No longer were people required to bring the blood of goats and bulls before God to obtain His forgiveness. The Lamb had been slain "to do away with sin by the sacrifice of himself" (Heb. 9:26). The perfect High Priest had finally come.

That's why today, you can bring your prayers to the water's edge, grasp the hand of the One who bridges the impossible gap between earth and eternity, and be ushered into the throne room of God with a standing appointment. Christ, our High Priest, has cleared the way.

> "God delights in hearing prayer and answering it. He gave His Son that Christ might always pray for us and with us."
>
> —Andrew Murray

NEXT UP — *You are part of a family who can trace its bloodline back two thousand years, to a hillside in Jerusalem—and to a place in the plan of God, dating back before time began.*

Notes

One Big Family

The People of God

Every color, every nation, every age and generation. We're not the world. We're the family of God.

Since you call on a Father who judges each man's work impartially, live your lives as strangers here in reverent fear. For you know that it was not with perishable things such as silver or gold that you were redeemed from the empty way of life handed down to you from your forefathers, but with the precious blood of Christ, a lamb without blemish or defect.

He was chosen before the creation of the world, but was revealed in these last times for your sake. Through him you believe in God, who raised him from the dead and glorified him, and so your faith and hope are in God.

Now that you have purified yourselves by obeying the truth so that you have sincere love for your brothers, love one another deeply, from the heart. For you have been born again, not of perishable seed, but of imperishable, through the living and enduring word of God. . . .

You are a chosen people, a royal priesthood, a holy nation, a people belonging to God, that you may declare the praises of him who called you out of darkness into his wonderful light. *Once you were not a people, but now you are the people of God*; once you had not received mercy, but now you have received mercy.

Scripture
1 Peter 1:18-23; 2:9-10

💫 DEFINING MOMENTS

Seems like everybody is entitled to free speech these days except the poor people who dare to suggest that God's ways are right and that His Word should still pull some weight around here. Christianity has been so maligned and caricatured, so scoffed and skewered, we're tempted at times to play dumb instead of speaking out. Why not just agree to disagree instead of offering our wrists to the razor blades of rejection? Nobody'd want to hear what we have to say anyway.

Now, listen up, you guys. We may be mistreated and misunderstood. But we're the people of God. We're thousands of years old and millions of people deep. We share faith with people in nearly every nation on the globe. And our core message has stood the test of time. The world may make fun of us to our face, but our gospel is still its only cure. They may paint us as phonies, but our peace is what they long for. They may dismiss us as unimportant, but our love will never die. We're the people of God. And we don't have to be afraid of this world. Or the next.

Notes

> "Christians are people whose activities are not so much determined by their past as they are by their future."
> —Timothy R. Phillips and Dennis L. Olkholm

NEXT UP *This world is not our home. We're strangers in a foreign land, aliens on a distant planet, ambassadors from a heavenly country. We are set apart to serve God's kingdom.*

Wholly Devoted

Consecration

When you became a
Christian, you gave up
your rights to citizenship.
But not to responsibility.

"I have revealed you to those whom you gave me out of the world. They were yours; you gave them to me and they have obeyed your word. Now they know that everything you have given me comes from you. For I gave them the words you gave me and they accepted them. They knew with certainty that I came from you, and they believed that you sent me.

"I pray for them. I am not praying for the world, but for those you have given me, for they are yours. . . .

"I will remain in the world no longer, but they are still in the world, and I am coming to you. Holy Father, protect them by the power of your name—the name you gave me—so that they may be one as we are one. . . .

"I am coming to you now, but I say these things while I am still in the world, so that they may have the full measure of my joy within them. I have given them your word and the world has hated them, for *they are not of the world any more than I am of the world*. My prayer is not that you take them out of the world but that you protect them from the evil one. They are not of the world, even as I am not of it."

Scripture

John 17:6-9, 11, 13-16

Notes

DEFINING MOMENTS

One world, two kingdoms: the kingdom of darkness and the kingdom of light. The spirit of the age and the God of the ages.

Those are your choices. And you've just made yours.

The problem is, though, that while your heart can be sold out to God, your feet must remain in the world—your eyes subject to its seductions, your ears within reach of its lies, your mind dangerously close to its deceptions. God has called you out from the world and its system of beliefs. He has set you apart, made you holy, consecrated you for His service. But He has plans for you while you're here. That's where the tightrope act comes in.

> "We are to keep the world from ruling our hearts by letting Christ rule there instead. The separation happens inside of us, not outside."
>
> —John Fischer

You'll be called on time and again to love the people of the world without being sucked into their way of thinking, to be an agent for cultural change without being changed to look like the culture, to relate to human need and speak human language without desiring human temptations. "In your hearts set apart Christ as Lord" (1 Pet. 3:15). And remember in Whose kingdom you're spoken for.

NEXT UP *You're a work in progress, just like the rest of us. You're not yet the person you want to be, but you're moving away from the one you were. Keep up the good work.*

In the Process

Sanctification

Finally, brothers, we instructed you how to live in order to please God, as in fact you are living. Now we ask you and urge you in the Lord Jesus to do this more and more. For you know what instructions we gave you by the authority of the Lord Jesus.

It is God's will that you should be sanctified: that you should avoid sexual immorality; that each of you should learn to control his own body in a way that is holy and honorable, not in passionate lust like the heathen, who do not know God; and that in this matter no one should wrong his brother or take advantage of him. The Lord will punish men for all such sins, as we have already told you and warned you.

For God did not call us to be impure, but to live a holy life. Therefore, he who rejects this instruction does not reject man but God, who gives you his Holy Spirit. . . .

Now the Lord is the Spirit, and where the Spirit of the Lord is, there is freedom. And we, who with unveiled faces all reflect the Lord's glory, are being transformed into his likeness with ever-increasing glory, which comes from the Lord, who is the Spirit.

Becoming a Christian is the first step in a long, joyful journey. And we're just getting a good start.

Scripture

1 Thessalonians 4:1-8;
2 Corinthians 3:17-18

⌇ DEFINING MOMENTS

What do you make of this long gap between the moment of your Christian conversion and the day you finally see its heavenly results? That leaves a lot of years in between unaccounted for, a lot of opportunities to either goof it up royally or to make good, steady progress.

What'll it be?

Welcome to the sanctification lab, where God's people get to try out the natural consequences of their beliefs—where the fresh fruit of patience meets the neighbor who reports your lawn to the community board, where the lofty words of integrity and holiness find themselves on the mean streets of temptation, where the easy prayers of blessing and joy can at times become a gut-wrenching cry for help.

> "The secret of Christian sanctity is not that we should strive to live like Jesus, but that He by His Spirit should come and live in us."
>
> —John R. W. Stott

In the midterm tests of life, God will change you from a person who says what he believes into a person who knows it from experience, from a person who can talk a good game into a person who can live it on or off the field—a person who's getting used to living with God.

NEXT UP *Growing deeper in Christ is not an automatic process, but a deliberate decision to learn what following God is all about. It's called discipleship. It's time to start.*

SEC7ION

Stepping Out on Faith

You've already walked the aisle into the outstretched

arms of your Savior. But your walking days have just begun.

Each day now presents you with a new opportunity to go one

more mile down the road, one leg closer to home, one jump

ahead of temptation—to see what freedom awaits you when

you let your Savior become your Lord.

Marching Orders

Discipleship

Disciples want nothing more than to be like their masters. Yours just happens to be the best there is.

To the Jews who had believed him, Jesus said, "If you hold to my teaching, you are really my disciples. Then you will know the truth, and the truth will set you free. . . ."

"Remain in me, and I will remain in you. No branch can bear fruit by itself; it must remain in the vine. Neither can you bear fruit unless you remain in me.

"I am the vine; you are the branches. *If a man remains in me and I in him, he will bear much fruit*; apart from me you can do nothing. If anyone does not remain in me, he is like a branch that is thrown away and withers; such branches are picked up, thrown into the fire and burned.

"If you remain in me and my words remain in you, ask whatever you wish, and it will be given you. This is to my Father's glory, that you bear much fruit, showing yourselves to be my disciples.

"As the Father has loved me, so have I loved you. Now remain in my love.

"If you obey my commands, you will remain in my love, just as I have obeyed my Father's commands and remain in his love. I have told you this so that my joy may be in you and that your joy may be complete."

Scripture

John 8:31-32; 15:4-11

⟳ DEFINING MOMENTS

You're going to find out very soon (if you haven't already) that the Christian life is no ice-cream social in the church basement. But for too many people, that's what they try to make it—a small-talk escape from the seriousness of the Sunday morning sermon, an opportunity to make an appearance as long as they're not asked to pray or anything.

If only it were that convenient to walk with Christ.

The call to discipleship goes out to every believer—no matter how old or far along on the journey—making an irrational appeal for you to come and die, to lay down everything you were and are on the altar of self-interests, and to "consider everything a loss compared to the surpassing greatness of knowing Christ Jesus my Lord" (Phil. 3:8).

> "Christianity without discipleship is Christianity without Christ. In such a religion there is trust in God, but no following of Christ."
> —Dietrich Bonhoeffer

But in return for this brave commitment, you receive a kind of life and depth that gives you purpose in place of potluck, passion instead of party games, and more opportunities to dish out Christian service than the lady who pours the punch. Are you hungry to be like Christ?

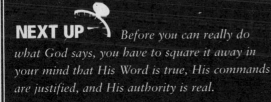

NEXT UP *Before you can really do what God says, you have to square it away in your mind that His Word is true, His commands are justified, and His authority is real.*

Just the Way It Is

Absolute Truth

So I will always remind you of these things, even though you know them and are firmly established in the truth you now have. . . .

And I will make every effort to see that after my departure you will always be able to remember these things.

We did not follow cleverly invented stories when we told you about the power and coming of our Lord Jesus Christ, but we were eyewitnesses of his majesty. For he received honor and glory from God the Father when the voice came to him from the Majestic Glory, saying, "This is my Son, whom I love; with him I am well pleased." We ourselves heard this voice that came from heaven when we were with him on the sacred mountain.

And we have the word of the prophets made more certain, and you will do well to pay attention to it, as to a light shining in a dark place, until the day dawns and the morning star rises in your hearts.

Above all, you must understand that no prophecy of Scripture came about by the prophet's own interpretation. For prophecy never had its origin in the will of man, but men spoke from God as they were carried along by the Holy Spirit.

Scripture

2 Peter 1:12, 15-21

> The truth is not the truth just because God says so. The truth is the truth because the truth is the truth.

⤷ DEFINING MOMENTS

Ask today's average Christians if they believe that the Bible represents the standard for personal morality, that it possesses absolute truth that applies to all people in all times and all places, and way too many of them will think you're taking this thing a little too far.

But despite the poll numbers, Christian disciples like you must realize that the Bible is your one and only authority on how to live.

The problem is: In this new age of personal expression, the subject of right and wrong has gone way out of style—even at times in Christian practice. The very idea that an invisible God can arbitrarily decide what someone should do in a given situation tramples too hard on individual freedom. "Doesn't the Constitution have some kind of protection against that?"

But if you choose to reject His Lordship, you slam the door—not only on what may be an unpopular demand or restriction, but on the freedom of living in union with the One who made you, who saved you, and who only wants what's best for you. And that's the truth.

Notes

> "Knowing what is right and wrong, we have a way to have order and freedom simultaneously."
>
> —Francis Schaeffer

NEXT UP *You're getting that look in your eye, that fire in your belly, that skip in your step that tells the world you've never been this serious about anything in your life.*

Awake at the Wheel

Spiritual Passion

There's only one way to live the Christian life right. And that's to do it with all you've got.

They devoted themselves to the apostles' teaching and to the fellowship, to the breaking of bread and to prayer. Everyone was filled with awe, and many wonders and miraculous signs were done by the apostles. All the believers were together and had everything in common. Selling their possessions and goods, they gave to anyone as he had need.

Every day they continued to meet together in the temple courts. They broke bread in their homes and ate together with glad and sincere hearts, praising God and enjoying the favor of all the people. And the Lord added to their number daily those who were being saved. . . .

All the believers were one in heart and mind. No one claimed that any of his possessions was his own, but they shared everything they had. With great power the apostles continued to testify to the resurrection of the Lord Jesus, and much grace was upon them all.

There were no needy persons among them. For from time to time those who owned lands or houses sold them, brought the money from the sales and put it at the apostles' feet, and it was distributed to anyone as he had need.

Scripture

Acts 2:42-47; 4:32-35

DEFINING MOMENTS

God's not looking for perfection, but for passion. He's not looking for people who are afraid to make a mistake, but for people who are just bold enough to make themselves look foolish if they have to in order to act out of genuine love and compassion. He's not nearly as concerned with the raunchy things you're avoiding as He is with the good and gracious things you're trusting Him to do through you.

Can you even begin to imagine the people you could reach with the good news of God's love if you could stop worrying about what others think and simply care about where they're headed? How many lives could you touch if you used your drive time to dream up ministry projects? How many situations could you have a hand in correcting if you replaced a mindless two-hour movie with a mighty two-hour prayer meeting? This is not some light-lunch pep talk. This is the hard-fought, rewarding reality that's yours to embrace as you start putting your passions where your faith is and living today in another world.

> "The Christian story is that of restoration of intimacy with God and the passion which comes from renewing our choice to respond to His wishes."
>
> —Gordon MacDonald

Notes

NEXT UP *But times will inevitably come when you're tempted to pull back, when failure and fatigue try to chain your faith to the floor. What happens when that happens?*

Sure of One Thing

Avoiding Disillusionment

When you feel the sleepy sighs of spiritual boredom coming on, stay where you can hear the alarm.

Therefore, since we are surrounded by such a great cloud of witnesses, let us throw off everything that hinders and the sin that so easily entangles, and *let us run with perseverance the race marked out for us.*

Let us fix our eyes on Jesus, the author and perfecter of our faith, who for the joy set before him endured the cross, scorning its shame, and sat down at the right hand of the throne of God. Consider him who endured such opposition from sinful men, so that you will not grow weary and lose heart. . . .

Make every effort to live in peace with all men and to be holy; without holiness no one will see the Lord. See to it that no one misses the grace of God and that no bitter root grows up to cause trouble and defile many.

See that no one is sexually immoral, or is godless like Esau, who for a single meal sold his inheritance rights as the oldest son. Afterward, as you know, when he wanted to inherit this blessing, he was rejected. He could bring about no change of mind, though he sought the blessing with tears. . . .

Therefore, since we are receiving a kingdom that cannot be shaken, let us be thankful, and so worship God acceptably with reverence and awe.

Scripture

Hebrews 12:1-3, 14-17, 28

DEFINING MOMENTS

You'll know you're growing as a Christian when the dry times come. Of course, you'll think you're doing just the opposite. You'll feel like a giant failure. Ashamed of yourself. A great big hypocrite.

But whether you've been blown into the desert by the scorching winds of sin or you've just found that the journey to the next oasis of spiritual victory is taking longer than you expected, now's your chance to build some muscle.

Will you keep your old habits from calling you out, from gunning you down with one blast of temptation? Or will you realize that in Christ you can play dead to sin no matter how bold its threats are?

Will you only move your feet when the fiery sands of spiritual thrills are making you feel like dancing? Or will you walk the faithful path beaten hard by earlier travelers, even when the road takes an uneventful stretch? Keep getting back up from your fall. Keep pouring your heart out for people who need what you've found. You'll look up one day and be amazed at what God's growing in you.

> "If you enter a dry season, don't treat your spiritual life casually. Christians who begin to treat Jesus casually often become casualties."
>
> —Tom Sirotnak

NEXT UP *You're not the only one who feels the way you do, who asks yourself questions or makes stupid mistakes. Try being honest with others about it. See what comes up.*

Notes

Oh, It's Just You

Being Yourself

But thanks be to God, who always leads us in triumphal procession in Christ and through us spreads everywhere the fragrance of the knowledge of him.

For we are to God the aroma of Christ among those who are being saved and those who are perishing. To the one we are the smell of death; to the other, the fragrance of life. And who is equal to such a task?

Unlike so many, we do not peddle the word of God for profit. On the contrary, in Christ *we speak before God with sincerity, like men sent from God.*

Are we beginning to commend ourselves again? Or do we need, like some people, letters of recommendation to you or from you? You yourselves are our letter, written on our hearts, known and read by everybody.

You show that you are a letter from Christ, the result of our ministry, written not with ink but with the Spirit of the living God, not on tablets of stone but on tablets of human hearts.

Such confidence as this is ours through Christ before God. Not that we are competent in ourselves to claim anything for ourselves, but our competence comes from God. He has made us competent as ministers of a new covenant.

Scripture

2 Corinthians 2:14-3:6

You'll waste a lot of opportunities to grow as a disciple if you pretend to be something you're not.

⟨ DEFINING MOMENTS

The villagers stood in awed, yet awkward silence—afraid to speak, to flinch, to look anyone in the eye for fear of seeming uncultured. While everything inside them was telling them to gasp, to point, to ask the one standing next to them if he saw what they were seeing, everything on the outside was smiles, nods, and applause—a war between honesty and appearances—until a boy too young to know any better shattered the strange stillness by giving voice to the very statement no one wanted to be the first to say.

"He has nothing on!" The emperor had no clothes.

Yet even though we don't live in a fairy-tale world, we are accustomed to being the villager on the street, avoiding the obvious, skirting the issue, appearing unfamiliar with others' problems that we know too well by heart, but never by admission.

Let's get real. Let's be honest. Let's not be satisfied with our sin, but let's not act like it's not there. Being an open book will give others the courage to be one themselves. And to find a true friend in need.

> "Many times our human desire to be acceptable to everyone keeps us from being real in all but the most superficial ways."
>
> —Jim Smoke

Notes

NEXT UP
One of the few people who knows your weak spots as well as you do is the devil. But you can learn how to use this inside knowledge to beat him at his own game.

Guard the Perimeter

Boundaries

You can paint temptation into a corner by sealing off its favorite points of entry into your life.

Do you not know that in a race all the runners run, but only one gets the prize? Run in such a way as to get the prize.

Everyone who competes in the games goes into strict training. They do it to get a crown that will not last; but we do it to get a crown that will last forever. Therefore I do not run like a man running aimlessly; I do not fight like a man beating the air. No, I beat my body and make it my slave so that after I have preached to others, I myself will not be disqualified for the prize. . . .

Those controlled by the sinful nature cannot please God. . . .

But if Christ is in you, your body is dead because of sin, yet your spirit is alive because of righteousness. And if the Spirit of him who raised Jesus from the dead is living in you, he who raised Christ from the dead will also give life to your mortal bodies through his Spirit, who lives in you.

Therefore, brothers, *we have an obligation—but it is not to the sinful nature,* to live according to it. For if you live according to the sinful nature, you will die; but if by the Spirit you put to death the misdeeds of the body, you will live.

Scripture
1 Corinthians 9:24-27;
Romans 8:8, 10-13

⚡ DEFINING MOMENTS

Notes

Test the logic in this. If you know you're going to be tempted to go for the potato chips while you watch the late news tonight, it'd be a good idea to keep them out of your pantry. If you know sexy, seductive pictures draw your eyes like a magnet, you probably shouldn't make a habit of shopping in the magazine aisle. If you know that every time you go over to this one friend's house, you always end up doing things you shouldn't, you'd be smart to not go over there.

> "Everything can be taken from a man but one thing: the last of human freedoms—to choose one's attitude in any given set of circumstances."
>
> —Viktor Frankl

Boundaries. They're lines that you draw in the sand of everyday life—as much to protect yourself as to put Satan on notice. Their self-imposed security alerts that warn you in advance of the areas he's most likely to strike. And when you team them up with promises you've made to accountability partners who are committed to watching your back for you, they can make you doubly difficult to defeat. They won't keep out all your temptations. The devil's never above a sneak attack. But they can shield you from the worst of it and give your integrity real staying power.

NEXT UP *But above changing the way you live and the things you choose to do, the process of discipleship can change the way you think about the important things in life.*

Needed at Home

Your Family

The most important people in the world are the ones God has placed right in your living room.

Wives, submit to your husbands as to the Lord. For the husband is the head of the wife as Christ is the head of the church, his body, of which he is the Savior. Now as the church submits to Christ, so also wives should submit to their husbands in everything.

Husbands, love your wives, just as Christ loved the church and gave himself up for her to make her holy, cleansing her by the washing with water through the word, and to present her to himself as a radiant church, without stain or wrinkle or any other blemish, but holy and blameless.

In this same way, husbands ought to love their wives as their own bodies. He who loves his wife loves himself. After all, no one ever hated his own body, but he feeds and cares for it, just as Christ does the church—for we are members of his body. . . .

Children, obey your parents in the Lord, for this is right. "Honor your father and mother"—which is the first commandment with a promise—"that it may go well with you and that you may enjoy long life on the earth." Fathers, do not exasperate your children; instead, *bring them up in the training and instruction of the Lord.*

Scripture

Ephesians 5:22-30; 6:1-4

ꙅ DEFINING MOMENTS

Your family is your proving ground, where early morning moods and unsightly closets leave no place for Christian beliefs to hide behind, no words to sugarcoat the bald-faced lives we lead when the outside world is out of earshot. Which can be a little scary.

But your family is also your training ground, where you can share life's most everyday challenges and experiences in the comfort of each other's company, where you can work through your shyness for bringing Sunday morning ideals into daily life by discovering how to pray as a family, how to use the Bible as a measuring stick, how to create a safe place for even the most childlike questions.

When Christ is given permission to make Himself at home at your house, you'll take pains to love your wife or husband more, to be more patient with your kids' mistakes, to be quicker to admit your own fault and to ask for forgiveness. You'll bite your tongue, you'll work for everyone's good, you'll give when you're tired and cranky. You'll grow. Together.

Notes

> "Whatever problems your family is facing, healing can and will take place if Jesus is allowed to come into your home and sit at the head of the table."
>
> —Robert and Debra Bruce

NEXT UP *And another thing that should look a little different through Christian eyes is the place where you work, the people you work with, the job that's expected of you.*

Always on the Job

Your Work

No longer is work or school just the necessary nightmare between you and a fun weekend.

We always thank God, the Father of our Lord Jesus Christ, when we pray for you, because we have heard of your faith in Christ Jesus and of the love you have for all the saints—the faith and love that spring from the hope that is stored up for you in heaven and that you have already heard about in the word of truth, the gospel that has come to you.

All over the world this gospel is bearing fruit and growing, just as it has been doing among you since the day you heard it and understood God's grace in all its truth. . . .

For this reason, since the day we heard about you, we have not stopped praying for you and asking God to fill you with the knowledge of his will through all spiritual wisdom and understanding.

And we pray this in order that you may live a life worthy of the Lord and may please him in every way: *bearing fruit in every good work, growing in the knowledge of God,* being strengthened with all power according to his glorious might so that you may have great endurance and patience, and joyfully giving thanks to the Father, who has qualified you to share in the inheritance of the saints in the kingdom of light.

Scripture

Colossians 1:3-6, 9-12

﹖ DEFINING MOMENTS

One important aspect of the Christian worldview is understanding the need for Christian men and women to be on the job in all kinds of workplaces and arenas—to be the "salt of the earth" and the "light of the world" in the courtroom and the classroom, on the assembly line and the executive office, in the public domain as well as the pulpit.

God has given each of us a calling in life. Some of those callings spill over very naturally into the kind of jobs we do. But in case you don't feel called to the work you're doing right now, yet you realize the necessity of it at this stage of your life, you can always remain in the will of God by striving for excellence in everything you do, caring genuinely for the people you serve and work alongside, looking for opportunities to offer Christian counsel and friendship, and maintaining integrity in all your relationships. You may have never seen anything very spiritual in turning a wrench, pecking a keyboard, or running another load of towels. But your faithful performance can speak volumes if you'll let it.

> "To follow Jesus means first and foremost to discover in our daily lives God's unique vocation for us."
>
> —Henri Nouwen

Notes

NEXT UP *Life puts you in contact with a lot of different people. Some are fun to be around. Some are a challenge. But God has put them all into your life for a reason.*

Building Bridges

Your Relationships

Friend or foe, relative or seemingly irrelevant, every person in your life is a ministry opportunity.

Love must be sincere. Hate what is evil; cling to what is good. Be devoted to one another in brotherly love. Honor one another above yourselves. Never be lacking in zeal, but keep your spiritual fervor, serving the Lord. Be joyful in hope, patient in affliction, faithful in prayer. Share with God's people who are in need. Practice hospitality.

Bless those who persecute you; bless and do not curse. Rejoice with those who rejoice; mourn with those who mourn. Live in harmony with one another. Do not be proud, but be willing to associate with people of low position. Do not be conceited.

Do not repay anyone evil for evil. Be careful to do what is right in the eyes of everybody. If it is possible, *as far as it depends on you, live at peace with everyone.*

Do not take revenge, my friends, but leave room for God's wrath, for it is written: "It is mine to avenge; I will repay," says the Lord. On the contrary: "If your enemy is hungry, feed him; if he is thirsty, give him something to drink. In doing this, you will heap burning coals on his head." Do not be overcome by evil, but overcome evil with good.

Scripture

Romans 12:9-21

↶ DEFINING MOMENTS

Every time you say hello to the ringing telephone, every time you open the door to dinner company, every time you plop your milk and bread up on the checkout conveyor, you get one more chance to have a godly influence on a buddy, a neighbor, a stranger. And the way you react in situations like these—be they casual, corporate, or confrontational—can paint honest, loving eyes on someone's personal picture of the Christ you serve.

It really is an awesome responsibility.

If God put us here for any other reason than to love and worship Him, it was to love and honor His children, to be a warm-eyed smile in a sea of grunts and frowns, a two-hour phone call in a world of busy signals, a lunch invitation in the middle of a long, lonely day.

Christian disciples are committed to lifting their friends a little higher, overlooking the faults of their enemies, and going out of their way to meet a need, remember a kindness, speak a word of encouragement. No one is insignificant to God or to the people who love Him.

Notes

> "If we will reach out to and hold on to each other, we will find companionship on our journey."
>
> –Sheila Walsh

NEXT UP *You have ears, you have eyes, you have time, you have television—you have all kinds of ways to get all kinds of stuff into your head. But only one way to control it.*

Heads Up

Your Thought Life

The biggest battle you'll face as a Christian will take place every day—right between your ears.

For though we live in the world, we do not wage war as the world does. The weapons we fight with are not the weapons of the world. On the contrary, they have divine power to demolish strongholds. We demolish arguments and every pretension that sets itself up against the knowledge of God, and we take captive every thought to make it obedient to Christ. . . .

Those who live according to the sinful nature have their minds set on what that nature desires; but those who live in accordance with the Spirit have their minds set on what the Spirit desires. The mind of sinful man is death, but *the mind controlled by the Spirit is life and peace.* . . .

So I say, live by the Spirit, and you will not gratify the desires of the sinful nature. . . .

Therefore, prepare your minds for action; be self-controlled; set your hope fully on the grace to be given you when Jesus Christ is revealed. As obedient children, do not conform to the evil desires you had when you lived in ignorance. But just as he who called you is holy, so be holy in all you do; for it is written: "Be holy, because I am holy."

Scripture

2 Corinthians 10:3-5; Romans 8:5-6; Galatians 5:16; 1 Peter 1:13-16

Notes

⟨ DEFINING MOMENTS

If you've ever wasted a whole evening trying to get to the bonus level on a video game, then you know what it's like to close your eyes at bedtime and see hostile, cartoon enemies sailing across the blank screen of your eyelids. That's because the thoughts you dwell on don't just come to visit. They come to stay. And if they're not the good kind, they can get to be very annoying company before they're done.

The same way a head cold makes your whole body feel lousy, the condition of your thought life affects your whole behavior. If you allow yourself to stew about the friend who mistreated you, you'll pass up lots of chances to mend your relationship. If you allow the movie screen to singe your ears with even more foul language than you already have to deal with at work, you'll start hearing it come out of your own mouth as well. But if you'll fill your mind with things that you know God would like and plug your ears to the devil's pack of lies, your feet will walk a straight line to spiritual success. And that's worth thinking about.

> "We must face the fact that a war is on. And unless we fight, how can we retake the fortresses of the enemy which are in the mind?"
>
> —Watchman Nee

NEXT UP *As your foundation starts to strengthen and feels firm to the touch, you can start putting on some new additions—nice little extras that can take your life to the next level.*

SECTION 8

Second Line of Defense

You'll never outgrow your basic need for the daily
nutritional requirements of Christian discipline—prayer,
Bible study, quiet time with the Lord. None of us do. But
God offers a lot more than bread and butter to satisfy your
hunger and to help you grow strong teeth and bones in your
spiritual life. Are you ready to dig in to dessert?

Going to Bat

Intercession

As you start praying for other people's problems, you'll become a lot less frightened of your own.

I urge, then, first of all, that requests, prayers, intercession and thanksgiving be made for everyone—for kings and all those in authority, that we may live peaceful and quiet lives in all godliness and holiness. This is good, and pleases God our Savior, who wants all men to be saved and to come to a knowledge of the truth.

For there is one God and one mediator between God and men, the man Christ Jesus, who gave himself as a ransom for all men—the testimony given in its proper time. . . .

In the same way, the Spirit helps us in our weakness. We do not know what we ought to pray for, but the Spirit himself intercedes for us with groans that words cannot express. And he who searches our hearts knows the mind of the Spirit, because the Spirit intercedes for the saints in accordance with God's will.

And we know that in all things God works for the good of those who love him, who have been called according to his purpose. . . .

Therefore confess your sins to each other and pray for each other so that you may be healed. *The prayer of a righteous man is powerful and effective.*

Scripture

1 Timothy 2:1-6; Romans 8:26-28; James 5:16

ᔐ DEFINING MOMENTS

My, my, my.

You don't have to look far to find enough personal matters to pray to God about. Between the new clutch that costs five hundred dollars that you don't have and the work that's due the day after tomorrow, between the sins that overtake you in the day and the worries that keep you up at night, you can talk God's ear off from now till next weekend and never get past your own little world.

But as surely as God cares about the things that concern you most (and loves to hear the sound of your voice turning to Him instead of shutting Him out), He wants to begin transforming your prayer life the same way He's changing you everywhere else: from the inside out, from self to service, from me to my neighbor.

God is making you into a person who really loves and cares. And as your heart for others begins spilling over into your prayer time, you'll be continually pleading their case before a higher court, sharing the load of their sufferings, and taking their hope in Him to new heights.

Notes

> "Talking to men for God is a great thing, but talking to God for men is still greater."
>
> —E. M. Bounds

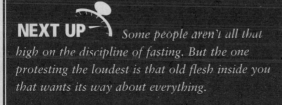

NEXT UP *Some people aren't all that high on the discipline of fasting. But the one protesting the loudest is that old flesh inside you that wants its way about everything.*

Breakfast of Champions

Fasting

Once you've gotten yourself filled up at God's table, you won't be hungry for anything else.

"When you fast, do not look somber as the hypocrites do, for they disfigure their faces to show men they are fasting. I tell you the truth, they have received their reward in full.

"But when you fast, put oil on your head and wash your face, so that it will not be obvious to men that you are fasting, but only to *your Father, who is unseen; and your Father, who sees what is done in secret, will reward you. . . .*"

"Is not this the kind of fasting I have chosen: to loose the chains of injustice and untie the cords of the yoke, to set the oppressed free and break every yoke? Is it not to share your food with the hungry and to provide the poor wanderer with shelter—when you see the naked, to clothe him, and not to turn away from your own flesh and blood?

"Then your light will break forth like the dawn, and your healing will quickly appear; then your righteousness will go before you, and the glory of the Lord will be your rear guard.

"Then you will call, and the Lord will answer; you will cry for help, and he will say: Here am I."

Scripture

Matthew 6:16-18;
Isaiah 58:6-9a

DEFINING MOMENTS

You may not think fasting is for you. After all, isn't it more of an advanced skill? Something more suited to those who have enough holiness in reserve to survive on forty days of tap water and beef broth?

Actually, fasting is for anyone who's ever felt squeezed by a pressing prayer concern, anyone who battles to keep his sinful self-will from calling the shots, anyone who's woken up in the morning with his head in a blur, unable to concentrate on one thought for two seconds without being bombarded by three more.

> "Fasting allows us to subordinate our body's needs to our spiritual need for God. It helps us to control our appetites before they control us."
>
> —James Houston

It's for everyone.

Try it for just one meal. Or one day. You can fast with lots of things besides just food, such as a certain food group you're struggling to avoid. Or the television. Or the Internet. Or the mall. Anything that's standing between you and pure, free-flowing fellowship with the Lord.

By starving the growling appetites of the flesh and devoting the time you save into quiet times of prayer, worship, and Bible reading, you'll find yourself renewed, refreshed, restored. Back in control.

NEXT UP *You may not like to think about harmful spiritual forces having you in their crosshairs. But you'd be delighted to know that you've got them outmanned.*

Notes

Braced for Battle

Spiritual Warfare

Go ahead and talk up where the devil can hear you. And remind him Who's fighting on your side.

Finally, be strong in the Lord and in his mighty power. Put on the full armor of God so that you can take your stand against the devil's schemes. *For our struggle is not against flesh and blood*, but against the rulers, against the authorities, against the powers of this dark world and against the spiritual forces of evil in the heavenly realms.

Therefore put on the full armor of God, so that when the day of evil comes, you may be able to stand your ground, and after you have done everything, to stand. Stand firm then, with the belt of truth buckled around your waist, with the breastplate of righteousness in place, and with your feet fitted with the readiness that comes from the gospel of peace.

In addition to all this, take up the shield of faith, with which you can extinguish all the flaming arrows of the evil one. Take the helmet of salvation and the sword of the Spirit, which is the word of God. And pray in the Spirit on all occasions with all kinds of prayers and requests. With this in mind, be alert and always keep on praying for all the saints.

Scripture
Ephesians 6:10-18

DEFINING MOMENTS

Even as marvelous and beyond description as God has created our minds and bodies, He has built into us certain restrictions to keep us from overloading on outside sensations and information. For instance, if we truly knew the staggering depths of human need around the world, our hearts couldn't contain the grief. If our ears could detect every sound signal that was waving at us across this very room, we would run screaming into the hills.

He knows that we can only withstand so much—which makes you wonder why He'd even mention the fact that we are being opposed this minute by "the powers of this dark world" and "the spiritual forces of evil in the heavenly realms" (Eph. 6:12). Seems like knowledge as horrific as that would fall under the "don't-need-to-know" category.

But God must have a reason for wanting us aware. He must want the devil to understand that we're wise to his schemes and us to understand that we have nothing to fear. With Christ leading the charge, we mere mortals can handle anything.

> "The devil is not frightened by our human efforts. But he knows his kingdom will be damaged when we lift our hearts up to God."
>
> —Jim Cymbala

Notes

NEXT UP *The life of Christ certainly doesn't paint a picture of giving up when faced with impossible circumstances. With the God who made it all, all things are possible.*

Only Believe

Miracles

After Jesus had finished instructing his twelve disciples, he went on from there to teach and preach in the towns of Galilee.

When John heard in prison what Christ was doing, he sent his disciples to ask him, "Are you the one who was to come, or should we expect someone else?"

Jesus replied, "Go back and report to John what you hear and see: The blind receive sight, the lame walk, those who have leprosy are cured, the deaf hear, the dead are raised, and the good news is preached to the poor. . . ."

"Don't you believe that I am in the Father, and that the Father is in me? The words I say to you are not just my own. Rather, it is the Father, living in me, who is doing his work. Believe me when I say that I am in the Father and the Father is in me; or at least believe on the evidence of the miracles themselves.

"I tell you the truth, anyone who has faith in me will do what I have been doing. He will do even greater things than these, because I am going to the Father. And I will do whatever you ask in my name, so that the Son may bring glory to the Father. *You may ask me for anything in my name, and I will do it.*"

Unless God was just buttering us up with wishful thinking, we have a right to trust Him for anything.

Scripture

Matthew 11:1-5;
John 14:10-14

⌇ DEFINING MOMENTS

You probably don't have any problem believing that miracles still occur in our day. You may even have enough faith to believe He'll perform one for you personally. The biggest problem we have with miracles is understanding why He does one for this person while overlooking another. It seems so random. So arbitrary. Not at all like the deliberate God of order and justice we've discovered Him to be.

But God does perform His miracles for a purpose—the same reason Christ performed them by the thousands while He ministered here on earth: so that "you may believe that Jesus is the Christ, and that by believing you may have life in his name" (John 20:31).

Healing cancer, saving lives, restoring relationships, providing cash flow, opening eyes, locating children, connecting people, salvaging ruin—these are only the entry points God uses to get through to people's hearts, to capture the attention of another skeptic, to lift the faith of another doubter, to turn the eyes of the lost to their only answer in life.

> "Signs do not take us away from reality. They are focal points at which more reality becomes visible to us than we ordinarily see all at once."
>
> —C. S. Lewis

NEXT UP — *If you're willing to open your mouth, God will give you the words to say—and an audience that He's already primed to hear what Jesus Christ has done for you.*

Notes

Share the Wealth

Witnessing

You have a story that'll speak volumes to someone. And a God who can put the two of you together.

Then Jesus came to them and said, "All authority in heaven and on earth has been given to me. Therefore go and make disciples of all nations, baptizing them in the name of the Father and of the Son and of the Holy Spirit, and teaching them to obey everything I have commanded you. And surely I am with you always, to the very end of the age. . . ."

Always be prepared to give an answer to everyone who asks you to give the reason for the hope that you have. But do this with gentleness and respect, keeping a clear conscience, so that those who speak maliciously against your good behavior in Christ may be ashamed of their slander. . . .

Devote yourselves to prayer, being watchful and thankful. And pray for us, too, that God may open a door for our message, so that we may proclaim the mystery of Christ, for which I am in chains. Pray that I may proclaim it clearly, as I should.

Be wise in the way you act toward outsiders; make the most of every opportunity. Let your conversation be always full of grace, seasoned with salt, so that you may know how to answer everyone.

Scripture

Matthew 28:18-20; 1 Peter 3:15b-16; Colossians 4:2-6

⤳ DEFINING MOMENTS

"How, then, can they call on the one they have not believed in? And how can they believe in the one of whom they have not heard? And how can they hear without someone preaching to them?" (Rom. 10:14).

He's got a point there.

But as logical as that sounds, you'll never have to look far to find an excuse to match. Either you're in too big of a hurry. Or you don't know your Bible well enough. You're not a good enough Christian to be talking. And you're pretty sure they're not interested anyway. Besides, you've got milk spoiling in the trunk.

But if you're ever able to realize that God can use you right where you are, that you're not personally responsible for how people take your word of witness, and that you can never know where the seed you plant today may lead tomorrow, you can feel free bringing God up in conversation anywhere He says. And trusting Him to get through to the people closest to you.

> Notes

> "Be willing to enter their world to tell them about Christ, rather than bringing them into your world before you talk."
>
> —John Kramp

NEXT UP *We all know that love is the unifying force which turns our faithfulness into effectiveness. But trailing along at a close second is another key ingredient: forgiveness.*

Under the Bridge

Forgiveness

You'll learn how to forgive, or you'll live a life of inadequate blessing and short-circuited ministry.

"The kingdom of heaven is like a king who wanted to settle accounts with his servants. As he began the settlement, a man who owed him ten thousand talents was brought to him. Since he was not able to pay, the master ordered that he and his wife and his children and all that he had be sold to repay the debt.

"The servant fell on his knees before him. 'Be patient with me,' he begged, 'and I will pay back everything.' The servant's master took pity on him, canceled the debt and let him go. "But when that servant went out, he found one of his fellow servants who owed him a hundred denarii. He grabbed him and began to choke him. 'Pay back what you owe me!' he demanded. "His fellow servant fell to his knees and begged him, 'Be patient with me, and I will pay you back.' But he refused. Instead, he went off and had the man thrown into prison until he could pay the debt. When the other servants saw what had happened, they were greatly distressed and went and told their master everything that had happened.

"Then the master called the servant in. 'You wicked servant,' he said, 'I canceled all that debt of yours because you begged me to. *Shouldn't you have had mercy on your fellow servant* just as I had on you?'"

Scripture

Matthew 18:23-33

Notes

☙ DEFINING MOMENTS

You know how much God loves to see you in church. He smiles the whole time you're tugging yourself out of bed on Sunday morning, splashing water in your face, grabbing a bagel or biscuit, and zooming down as fast as you can to soak up the fellowship, enter into praise, and hear the Word explained and experienced in the flow of worship. Throw in Sunday and Wednesday nights, and you're a long way toward getting your Christian priorities in apple-pie order.

But knowing how important that church attendance and involvement are in your overall spiritual health, it's worth listening carefully when Jesus says, "If you are offering your gift at the altar and there remember that your brother has something against you, leave your gift there in front of the altar. First go and be reconciled with your brother; then come and offer your gift" (Matt. 5:23-24).

Your life will stay fairly empty and you'll strain to be free to worship and serve if you don't give forgiveness the chance to come first.

> "Our principal weapon in the crises we face in the world is love, and love operates only in a state of reconciliation and forgiveness."
>
> —Pat Robertson

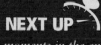

NEXT UP *One of the most holy moments in the entire Christian experience is the observance of Communion or the Lord's Supper. Don't miss its deeper messages.*

Bread of Life

Communion

Every time you receive the bread and the wine, you're a witness to life's most incredible mystery.

For I received from the Lord what I also passed on to you: The Lord Jesus, on the night he was betrayed, took bread, and when he had given thanks, he broke it and said, *"This is my body, which is for you; do this in remembrance of me."* In the same way, after supper he took the cup, saying, "This cup is the new covenant in my blood; do this, whenever you drink it, in remembrance of me." For whenever you eat this bread and drink this cup, you proclaim the Lord's death until he comes.

Therefore, whoever eats the bread or drinks the cup of the Lord in an unworthy manner will be guilty of sinning against the body and blood of the Lord. A man ought to examine himself before he eats of the bread and drinks of the cup. For anyone who eats and drinks without recognizing the body of the Lord eats and drinks judgment on himself.

That is why many among you are weak and sick, and a number of you have fallen asleep. But if we judged ourselves, we would not come under judgment. When we are judged by the Lord, we are being disciplined so that we will not be condemned with the world.

Scripture
1 Corinthians 11:23-32

⚡ DEFINING MOMENTS

On a crisp November noonday, a gray-haired gentleman in a navy blue vinyl windbreaker stands at solemn attention—one hand over his heart, the other brushing away a noble tear—just like every year at the Veteran's Day parade. Yet a block away, a frazzled young businessman darts his car through alleys and side roads, barking his disbelief at why they'd tie up a main downtown street like this at lunchtime.

The only reason that customs and traditions wither into meaningless ritual is because we forget or don't understand what they represent. But when we eat the bread and drink from the cup of Communion, we're joining with millions of fellow believers across centuries and time zones, affirming our common faith and remembering the price of our salvation. We're renewing our commitment to holy living and piling up our forgiven sins at the base of the cross. And we're getting just a taste of the celebration that's in store when we gather around heaven's table at the "wedding supper of the Lamb" (Rev. 19:9). Come and dine.

> "The Lord's Supper is memorative, and so it has the nature and use of a pledge or token of love, left by a dying man to a dear surviving friend. It is like a ring plucked off from Christ's finger, or a bracelet from His arm, or rather His picture from His breast."
>
> —John Flavel

NEXT UP ➤ *In order for you to be all that God wants you to become, you'll need much more than a sturdy resolve. You'll need the Holy Spirit of God in large doses.*

More and More

Being Spirit-Filled

God has a way of leading you that's better than anything you can come up with on your own.

The sinful nature desires what is contrary to the Spirit, and the Spirit what is contrary to the sinful nature. They are in conflict with each other, so that you do not do what you want. But if you are led by the Spirit, you are not under law.

The acts of the sinful nature are obvious: sexual immorality, impurity and debauchery; idolatry and witchcraft; hatred, discord, jealousy, fits of rage, selfish ambition, dissensions, factions and envy; drunkenness, orgies, and the like. I warn you, as I did before, that those who live like this will not inherit the kingdom of God.

But the fruit of the Spirit is love, joy, peace, patience, kindness, goodness, faithfulness, gentleness and self-control. Against such things there is no law. Those who belong to Christ Jesus have crucified the sinful nature with its passions and desires. *Since we live by the Spirit, let us keep in step with the Spirit. . . .*

Jesus stood and said in a loud voice, "If anyone is thirsty, let him come to me and drink. Whoever believes in me, as the Scripture has said, streams of living water will flow from within him." By this he meant the Spirit, whom those who believed in him were later to receive.

Scripture

Galatians 5:17-25;
John 7:37b-39

∽ DEFINING MOMENTS

Yes, there is a way to operate your car without the benefit of gas. You can throw it in neutral, open the driver's side door, heave with all the isometric power you can generate from your knees and shoulders, and at least creep it to the side of the road to avoid being smashed by moving traffic. You won't go far. You won't go fast. And even if you're able to keep it rolling for a little while, you'll eventually come to a steep enough incline to bring all your hard work to a weary halt.

> "The way to cultivate true graces of character is by submitting ourselves utterly to the Spirit to do His work and to bear His fruit."
>
> —R. A. Torrey

That's life in the slow lane—life without the Holy Spirit's power animating your actions, injecting your mind with spiritual insights, driving you to acts of unselfish love and kindness, steering you toward people in need of God's tender touch.

If you don't want to stay stranded on the shoulder of the Christian road, offer the Spirit a clean car to drive. And let Him take you for a joy ride to your chosen destination, keeping your tank filled with supreme purpose, your steps in perfect balance and alignment, your engine running on all cylinders.

NEXT UP *If you want to receive the blessings of God's continual presence, you'll also have to accept His right to offer correction and rebuke. It's for your own good. Honest.*

I Needed That

God's Chastening

God will clip the wings on your freedom at times, in order to help you learn what true freedom is.

You have forgotten that word of encouragement that addresses you as sons:

"My son, do not make light of the Lord's discipline, and do not lose heart when he rebukes you, because the Lord disciplines those he loves, and he punishes everyone he accepts as a son."

Endure hardship as discipline; God is treating you as sons. For what son is not disciplined by his father? If you are not disciplined (and everyone undergoes discipline), then you are illegitimate children and not true sons. Moreover, we have all had human fathers who disciplined us and we respected them for it. How much more should we submit to the Father of our spirits and live!

Our fathers disciplined us for a little while as they thought best; but *God disciplines us for our good, that we may share in his holiness.*

No discipline seems pleasant at the time, but painful. Later on, however, it produces a harvest of righteousness and peace for those who have been trained by it.

Therefore, strengthen your feeble arms and weak knees.

Scripture
Hebrews 12:5-12

⟨ DEFINING MOMENTS

Fathers are known for buying you ice cream and bubble gum, giving you rides on their shoulders, and teaching you how to tie a good square knot.

But fathers are also known for the belt, for the late-night questions about why you've been coming in so late, and for grounding you for a month to make sure it doesn't happen again.

Fathers who care are willing to watch you hurt, if temporary pain can save you from long-term disaster. Fathers who care are willing to watch you fall, if a sore spot on your pride can make you walk a little more carefully. Fathers who care are willing to interfere with your fun, if a word of warning can teach you that life's not a game.

And your Father cares—enough to let you face the consequences of your sin, to let you feel the pain you've caused another person, to allow things into your life that overpower your inner reserves, so that like a toddler in the deep end, you'll cry out for Daddy. And learn that you can trust Him.

> "Until we accept the fact that our Father is willing to discipline us, we'll never be able to comprehend what He's doing in our lives."
>
> —James Lucas

Notes

NEXT UP  *Your house is His. Your car is His. Your money is His. Your family is His. Every single thing you have is His. You're just taking care of it for Him. Aren't you?*

Something Borrowed

Stewardship

God is awfully generous to let us borrow all these things. Are you willing to start giving them back?

"Do not store up for yourselves treasures on earth, where moth and rust destroy, and where thieves break in and steal. But store up for yourselves treasures in heaven, where moth and rust do not destroy, and where thieves do not break in and steal. *For where your treasure is, there your heart will be also.* . . .

"No one can serve two masters. Either he will hate the one and love the other, or he will be devoted to the one and despise the other. You cannot serve both God and Money. . . ."

Command those who are rich in this present world not to be arrogant nor to put their hope in wealth, which is so uncertain, but to put their hope in God, who richly provides us with everything for our enjoyment. Command them to do good, to be rich in good deeds, and to be generous and willing to share.

In this way they will lay up treasure for themselves as a firm foundation for the coming age, so that they may take hold of the life that is truly life.

Scripture

Matthew 6:19-21, 24;
1 Timothy 6:17-19

Notes

⎰ DEFINING MOMENTS

In church vocabulary, stewardship is usually code for a fund drive. But it actually cheapens the principle of Christian stewardship to limit its scope to just money. As a committed disciple of Jesus Christ, you're in charge of mountains of blessings that are yours to use, share, and invest—but never to own.

Money is certainly one of them. But so is your time and your entire package of talents and abilities. Even the words you say and the health you enjoy are gifts from the hand of God that each require careful attention, wise handling, and (at times) measured restraint.

> "A good steward recognizes the value of what he possesses, and wisely manages it to the glory of the one who owns it."
>
> —Jack Taylor

And as you prove your faithfulness in managing small portions of God's resources, don't be surprised to see Him commit even more into your care, knowing that He can trust you to manage His property and be a funnel for passing the blessing along to others— the same way He's passed it along to you.

Money can't go to your head when you have God's interests at heart.

NEXT UP *Christian living comes with a lot of challenges like these, but life's not easy for anybody. Why not at least let your challenges pay off the way yours are going to?*

SECTION

From Here to Eternity

You can't really accuse God of false advertising. He used the
same size print to discuss the difficult parts of Christian living
as He did for the attractive ones. But when it comes to letting
us know about what heaven is like and the prizes we get just
for being His child, you can be sure He's not telling us
everything. That would take a much bigger book.

Value Judgments

Choosing Wisely

Sometimes your choices are not between right and wrong, but between good, better, and best.

At Gibeon the Lord appeared to Solomon during the night in a dream, and God said, "Ask for whatever you want me to give you."

Solomon answered, "You have shown great kindness to your servant, my father David, because he was faithful to you and righteous and upright in heart. You have continued this great kindness to him and have given him a son to sit on his throne this very day.

"Now, O Lord my God, you have made your servant king in place of my father David. But I am only a little child and do not know how to carry out my duties. Your servant is here among the people you have chosen, a great people, too numerous to count or number. So give your servant a discerning heart to govern your people and to distinguish between right and wrong. For who is able to govern this great people of yours?"

The Lord was pleased that Solomon had asked for this. So God said to him, "Since you have asked for this and not for long life or wealth for yourself, nor have asked for the death of your enemies but for discernment in administering justice, I will do what you have asked. *I will give you a wise and discerning heart.*"

Scripture

1 Kings 3:5-12

⚡ DEFINING MOMENTS

You can avoid the pain of countless regrets, disappoint yourself (and others) much less frequently, and keep your daily schedule from running your life out of control by memorizing this simple response:

No.

There—you said it. Of course, it wasn't easy. It may have meant you had to pick the library over your Sunday School class picnic this Saturday, or stay up an extra two hours tonight to make time for your child's Little League game this afternoon, or finish up your small-group Bible study homework instead of watching the Cubs on TV. But those are the choices you have to make if you want to be the person God's grooming you to be—the person you see in your mind's eye when a sermon hits home or a book speaks right to you. Learning to say no to the good and OK to the better option that's on the table will move you light years ahead on your Christian journey—leaving you free to enjoy the ride. And to make sure you're traveling at God's steady pace.

> "We are free to say no to good opportunities in order to say yes to the best, to do a few things without feeling we have to do everything."
>
> —Peg Rankin

Notes

NEXT UP *The issue is priorities—having a deliberate framework in place to help you make good decisions, avoid lazy distractions, and increase your inclination to obey.*

Living on Purpose

Priorities

When you know who you are, and you know where you're going, you can live for God like you mean it.

Do your best to present yourself to God as one approved, a workman who does not need to be ashamed and who correctly handles the word of truth. . . .

In a large house there are articles not only of gold and silver, but also of wood and clay; some are for noble purposes and some for ignoble. If a man cleanses himself from the latter, he will be an instrument for noble purposes, made holy, useful to the Master and prepared to do any good work. . . .

My son, pay attention to what I say; listen closely to my words.

Do not let them out of your sight, keep them within your heart; for they are life to those who find them and health to a man's whole body.

Above all else, guard your heart, for it is the wellspring of life.

Put away perversity from your mouth; keep corrupt talk far from your lips.

Let your eyes look straight ahead, fix your gaze directly before you.

Make level paths for your feet and take only ways that are firm. Do not swerve to the right or the left; keep your foot from evil.

Scripture

2 Timothy 2:15, 20-21;
Proverbs 4:20-27

⎨ **DEFINING MOMENTS**

Vision statements, core values, guiding principles. That's what you hear today's CEOs talking about in their board meetings and sales conferences—overarching themes that help workers evaluate their daily decisions in the light of well-thought-out criteria.

And it works—because when you can size up a situation based on something more than an immediate hunch, you can stay true to your goals and watch them take shape before your very eyes.

That's why every Christian needs to take the time to map out his personal priorities concerning faith, family, calling, careers, and daily life. Prayerful priorities can help you manage your time more productively, weigh the costs of your promises and commitments, and thwart the world's attempts at keeping you trivially minded when God wants you dealing in much more important things.

Left to itself, your life will tend to deteriorate. But led by the Spirit, you can move through life on a mission—and make it all the way.

> "Christianity, if false, is of no importance, and if true, is of infinite importance. The one thing it cannot be is moderately important."
>
> —C. S. Lewis

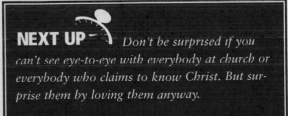

NEXT UP — *Don't be surprised if you can't see eye-to-eye with everybody at church or everybody who claims to know Christ. But surprise them by loving them anyway.*

Above the Fray

Unity in Diversity

You won't like every person you meet in this family. But with God's help, you can learn to get along.

The body is a unit, though it is made up of many parts; and though all its parts are many, they form one body. So it is with Christ. *For we were all baptized by one Spirit into one body—* whether Jews or Greeks, slave or free—and we were all given the one Spirit to drink. . . .

In fact God has arranged the parts in the body, every one of them, just as he wanted them to be. . . .

The eye cannot say to the hand, "I don't need you!" And the head cannot say to the feet, "I don't need you!" On the contrary, those parts of the body that seem to be weaker are indispensable, and the parts that we think are less honorable we treat with special honor. And the parts that are unpresentable are treated with special modesty, while our presentable parts need no special treatment.

But God has combined the members of the body and has given greater honor to the parts that lacked it, so that there should be no division in the body, but that its parts should have equal concern for each other.

If one part suffers, every part suffers with it; if one part is honored, every part rejoices with it.

Scripture

1 Corinthians 12:12-13, 18, 21-26

DEFINING MOMENTS

When you first come to Christ, it almost seems like a dream world. Everybody's so nice, so accepting, so quick to shake your hand and take an interest in your life. But the longer you hang around, and the more you discover about the people of God—even the ones who worship on the seat right next to you—you'll find that we have a lot of differences. Different backgrounds. Different callings. Different opinions and expectations. And getting all those differences to mesh into one unified body can be a stretch on our relating skills.

Enter the Holy Spirit—whose powerful capacity to love can fill your heart with patience and grace, helping you give people the freedom to live within their own temperaments, to move at their own pace, to express their own reasons for holding their particular brand of beliefs.

C. S. Lewis wrote, "When all is said about the divisions of Christendom, there remains by God's mercy an enormous common ground." And if you can learn to be happy with that, you'll be one happy person.

> "As long as our knowledge is imperfect, our preferences vary, and our opinions differ, let's leave a lot of room in areas that don't really matter."
>
> —Charles Swindoll

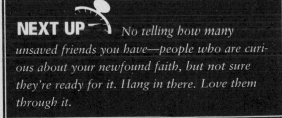

NEXT UP *No telling how many unsaved friends you have—people who are curious about your newfound faith, but not sure they're ready for it. Hang in there. Love them through it.*

Loved to Life

Being Patient with the Unsaved

The Lord waited on you for a pretty long time. How long are you willing to wait on your friends?

You, therefore, have no excuse, you who pass judgment on someone else, for at whatever point you judge the other, you are condemning yourself, because you who pass judgment do the same things.

Now we know that God's judgment against those who do such things is based on truth. So when you, a mere man, pass judgment on them and yet do the same things, do you think you will escape God's judgment? Or *do you show contempt for the riches of his kindness*, tolerance and patience, not realizing that God's kindness leads you toward repentance? . . .

For God does not show favoritism. . . .

"Do not judge, or you too will be judged. For in the same way as you judge others, you will be judged, and with the measure you use, it will be measured to you. . . ."

But do not forget this one thing, dear friends: With the Lord a day is like a thousand years, and a thousand years are like a day. The Lord is not slow in keeping his promise, as some understand slowness. He is patient with you, not wanting anyone to perish, but everyone to come to repentance.

Scripture

Romans 2:1-4, 11; Matthew 7:1-2; 2 Peter 3:8-9

⟲ DEFINING MOMENTS

The hang-ups are so much more real today. Barely a person alive hasn't felt at least a glancing blow from abuse, abandonment, divorce, disillusionment. Even some people who appear to be coasting through life can be casualties of cynicism or trying hard to hide the undertow of their own self-esteem. They find it hard to accept why God is the way He is. And if He even is at all, what would make Him want to love people like them?

That's why even people who may be hungry for the things you've found aren't likely to believe everything you say. They need to see it in your life. They need to see it with your time. They need to see it when it's not convenient or acceptable, but when it shows how much you care about their needs and concerns.

It may take months. It may take years. It may not ever click at all. But are you willing to let God lead you to the ones He's wanting nearer? Are you willing to invest yourself in the life of another person? Are you willing to go the extra mile to keep a friend from turning back?

> "Our aim is not to force people to live like Christians, but to persuade them to consider Christ."
>
> —John Fischer

NEXT UP *Not every person in need of your Christian witness is at work or around the corner. The ones you'll have the best chance of reaching are the ones right in your own home.*

Passing the Torch

Discipling Our Children

Let's never be so busy taking our message to the world that we forget the little ones right at our feet.

Love the Lord your God with all your heart and with all your soul and with all your strength. These commandments that I give you today are to be upon your hearts. Impress them on your children. Talk about them when you sit at home and when you walk along the road, when you lie down and when you get up.

Tie them as symbols on your hands and bind them on your foreheads. Write them on the doorframes of your houses and on your gates. . . .

We will not hide them from their children; *we will tell the next generation the praiseworthy deeds of the Lord*, his power, and the wonders he has done.

He decreed statutes for Jacob and established the law in Israel, which he commanded our forefathers to teach their children, so the next generation would know them, even the children yet to be born, and they in turn would tell their children.

Then they would put their trust in God and would not forget his deeds but would keep his commands. . . .

Even when I am old and gray, do not forsake me, O God, till I declare your power to the next generation, your might to all who are to come.

Scripture

Deuteronomy 6:5-9;
Psalm 78:4-7; 71:18

DEFINING MOMENTS

You only get them for a few years. Ask someone who's already watched theirs grow up and leave the nest, and you'll find out in a hurry how fast the time flies. They're eighteen, they're twenty-five, they've got children of their own, but in the mind's eye of a Mom or Dad, they should still need a phone book to sit up tall at the table.

So big. So fast. Kind of chokes you up just thinking about it.

So now's your chance to lay the groundwork for a child God's depending on you to mold. No matter how busy you are with the rest of your life, no matter how unaccustomed you are to talking spiritual things in front of your family, you're being counted on to model Christ to your little boy or girl, to be the picture they get of loving authority, to be the safe place they can turn for an honest answer, to be the living evidence that all this church talk really does carry over into everyday life.

Help them learn to submit their will to yours today, so that when they're out there on their own, they'll be able to submit to God's.

> "If we abandon our vision for our children, we are left to wander aimlessly with no direction other than our own self-interest."
>
> —Susan Card

NEXT UP *One of the most powerful lifestyles you can adopt is the freedom of letting God's blessings flow through you into the lives of others. Generosity looks good on everyone.*

Openhanded

Generosity

When you hold on too tightly to what's yours, you miss the whole point of why God gave it to you.

Remember this: Whoever sows sparingly will also reap sparingly, and *whoever sows generously will also reap generously.*

Each man should give what he has decided in his heart to give, not reluctantly or under compulsion, for God loves a cheerful giver. And God is able to make all grace abound to you, so that in all things at all times, having all that you need, you will abound in every good work. . . .

Now he who supplies seed to the sower and bread for food will also supply and increase your store of seed and will enlarge the harvest of your righteousness. You will be made rich in every way so that you can be generous on every occasion, and through us your generosity will result in thanksgiving to God.

This service that you perform is not only supplying the needs of God's people but is also overflowing in many expressions of thanks to God.

Because of the service by which you have proved yourselves, men will praise God for the obedience that accompanies your confession of the gospel of Christ, and for your generosity in sharing with them and with everyone else.

Scripture

2 Corinthians 9:6-8, 10-13

DEFINING MOMENTS

You haven't lived until you've looked into the impoverished eyes of a homeless person and offered him the sack lunch you'd made for yourself that morning. You haven't lived until you've sensed God stirring you to give one hundred dollars to a young couple in your church and heard them tell you how hard they'd been praying for that exact same amount. You haven't lived until you've learned that giving is a privilege, giving is contagious.

Giving is fun.

Just take the ten percent (the tithe) that God asks you to invest in your church. Most people feel good about tossing a five or a few ones in the offering plate—as though they were giving God a tip. But how can you feel satisfied tossing your Master a bone after all He's faithfully done for you—after He's been keeping you up in clothes, your breakfast cereal in the pantry, your heart beating like a drum sixty times a minute. It's not a chore to pour as much as possible back into His kingdom so that others can enjoy the same things you do. It's an honor. It's a joy. Try it. You'll see.

> "Giving from a grateful heart and expecting nothing in return is a sweet offering to the One who owns everything you have anyway."
>
> —Mary Hunt

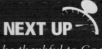

NEXT UP *But of all the things you can be thankful to God for, what about the freedom of knowing that death is but a door, that your reward is waiting—just on the other side?*

Notes

Grave Misgivings

Victory Over Death

> The devil can scream and holler and stamp his feet all he wants to. He can't have this little soul.

The body that is sown is perishable, it is raised imperishable; it is sown in dishonor, it is raised in glory; it is sown in weakness, it is raised in power; it is sown a natural body, it is raised a spiritual body. . . .

Listen, I tell you a mystery: We will not all sleep, but we will all be changed—in a flash, in the twinkling of an eye, at the last trumpet. For the trumpet will sound, the dead will be raised imperishable, and we will be changed.

For the perishable must clothe itself with the imperishable, and the mortal with immortality. When the perishable has been clothed with the imperishable, and the mortal with immortality, then the saying that is written will come true: "Death has been swallowed up in victory."

"Where, O death, is your victory? *Where, O death, is your sting?*"

The sting of death is sin, and the power of sin is the law. But thanks be to God! He gives us the victory through our Lord Jesus Christ.

Therefore, my dear brothers, stand firm. Let nothing move you. Always give yourselves fully to the work of the Lord, because you know that your labor in the Lord is not in vain.

Scripture

1 Corinthians 15:42b-44a, 51-58

৻ DEFINING MOMENTS

Jonathan was just eight. Barely tall enough to stretch to the top of the red stick that cleared him to ride the big roller coaster. We'd been pumping him all day: "You sure you want to go? It's really scary."

His words said yes. His eyes said he wasn't so sure.

He handed over his ball cap to Mom for safekeeping and took his place with Dad in the turnstiles. Inch by inch, they worked closer and closer, his laugh getting more nervous, his feet and hands a constant fidget.

> "Long did we seek you, freedom—in discipline, action, and suffering. Now that we die, in the face of God Himself we behold you."
>
> —Dietrich Bonhoeffer

Before long, the fear was all over his face. "We can go back, son. It's all right." But with a stiff shake of his head, they were locked into the car. His face was white. His knuckles clenched. For the longest 45 seconds of his young life, he clung somewhere between guts and glory—holding his breath through every dip, closing his eyes on the ratchety inclines, until it jerked to a halt back in the station, his odyssey complete. "That wasn't so bad. Thanks for taking me, Dad."

Death must be like that. It's not so bad. Thanks for taking us, Dad.

NEXT UP *Even when life scratches us hard enough to break the skin, we have hope— hope that no defeat is ever final. We have hope. We have hope. We still have hope.*

Going Home

Heaven

Heaven is more real than the room you're sitting in. You can stand anything with that in your future.

Then I saw a new heaven and a new earth, for the first heaven and the first earth had passed away, and there was no longer any sea. I saw the Holy City, the new Jerusalem, coming down out of heaven from God, prepared as a bride beautifully dressed for her husband.

And I heard a loud voice from the throne saying, "Now the dwelling of God is with men, and he will live with them. They will be his people, and God himself will be with them and be their God.

He will wipe every tear from their eyes. There will be no more death or mourning or crying or pain, for the old order of things has passed away."

He who was seated on the throne said, "I am making everything new!" Then he said, "Write this down, for these words are trustworthy and true."

He said to me: "It is done. I am the Alpha and the Omega, the Beginning and the End. To him who is thirsty I will give to drink without cost from the spring of the water of life. *He who overcomes will inherit all this, and I will be his God* and he will be my son. . . ."

Scripture

Revelation 21:1-7

Ꮹ **DEFINING MOMENTS**

"You've got your Christian model and your non-Christian model. Those are the only two kinds we carry."

"Well, just looking on the outside, they appear to be pretty similar. What's the difference between the two?"

"Uh, you're exactly right. They are very similar. Both have healthy bodies. Both have nice-looking families. Both come equipped with the usual house, car, paying job, microwave, etc."

"OK. But isn't there anything different about them?"

"Well, the Christian model claims to come with more peace of mind and a lot more power. But those who've tried the non-Christian model think it's all in their head. Of course, on the other hand, people have told us that the non-Christian brand doesn't seem to hold up as well as the other one. And the warranty is a lot more vague and unreliable. All in all, I'd say that's the biggest difference. The non-Christian has no promises to fall back on. But the Christian has hope. If I were you, I think I'd go with that one."

> "To pretend to describe heaven by the most artful composition of words would be but to darken and cloud it."
>
> —Jonathan Edwards

Notes

NEXT UP *Jesus Christ is coming back to earth through a real sky on a real day to take a real people to a real paradise. Wouldn't you really like to be here to see that?*

Encore! Encore!

Christ's Return

Just as surely as you believe He lay in a manger, He's going to peel back the sky and leap in to save us.

Brothers, we do not want you to be ignorant about those who fall asleep, or to grieve like the rest of men, who have no hope. We believe that Jesus died and rose again and so we believe that God will bring with Jesus those who have fallen asleep in him.

According to the Lord's own word, we tell you that we who are still alive, who are left till the coming of the Lord, will certainly not precede those who have fallen asleep. For the Lord himself will come down from heaven, with a loud command, with the voice of the archangel and with the trumpet call of God, and the dead in Christ will rise first.

After that, we who are still alive and are left will be caught up together with them in the clouds to meet the Lord in the air. And so we will be with the Lord for ever. Therefore encourage each other with these words.

Now, brothers, about times and dates we do not need to write to you, for you know very well that *the day of the Lord will come like a thief in the night.* . . .

But you, brothers, are not in darkness so that this day should surprise you like a thief. . . . So then, let us not be like others, who are asleep, but let us be alert and self-controlled.

Scripture

1 Thessalonians 4:13-5:2, 4, 6

DEFINING MOMENTS

Through no fault of our own, really, we're so acclimated to this earth that at times the thought of Christ's return makes us wish He'd hold off for a while. We want to see our children marry. We want to take our grandkids out for pizza. We want to see our business flourish, get a home in the country, finally work our way up to a marathon, see the tulip bulbs bloom out in the spring, enjoy the only life that we know.

"Somewhere, somewhen, somehow, we who are worshiping God here will wake up to see Him as He is, face to face."

—John Baillie

If we only knew.

Christ's coming to earth will be more glorious than anything we've ever experienced—more thrilling than Game Six of the '75 World Series, more exhilarating than the chill of a mountain spring in summertime, more beautiful than your wife's eyes behind her wedding veil. We will see Him—yes, Him!—Jesus, the Lamb of God, the Lord of glory, the Lover of our souls—face to face, eye to eye, as though He's just been dying for the day to come when He could hold us in His arms, wrap us in His love, and take us safely home to the glorious place He's made for us. Come quickly, Lord Jesus!

NEXT UP *They can make us breathe the air down here. They can make us drink the water. But they can't make our hearts feel at home anymore. We belong somewhere else.*

Notes

What a Finish

Glory

Since, then, you have been raised with Christ, set your hearts on things above, where Christ is seated at the right hand of God. Set your minds on things above, not on earthly things. *For you died, and your life is now hidden with Christ in God.* When Christ, who is your life, appears, then you also will appear with him in glory. . . .

In his great mercy he has given us new birth into a living hope through the resurrection of Jesus Christ from the dead, and into an inheritance that can never perish, spoil or fade—kept in heaven for you, who through faith are shielded by God's power until the coming of the salvation that is ready to be revealed in the last time.

In this you greatly rejoice, though now for a little while you may have had to suffer grief in all kinds of trials. These have come so that your faith—of greater worth than gold, which perishes even though refined by fire—may be proved genuine and may result in praise, glory and honor when Jesus Christ is revealed.

Though you have not seen him, you love him; and even though you do not see him now, you believe in him and are filled with an inexpressible and glorious joy, for you are receiving the goal of your faith, the salvation of your souls.

If people say you've got your head in the clouds, tell them not to knock it till they've been there.

Scripture

Colossians 3:1-4;
1 Peter 1:3b-9

⟨ DEFINING MOMENTS

Life looks different through the eyes of eternity.

The game can be played without your son getting to start. The dirty laundry won't kill anyone if it's not cleaned till tomorrow. The meeting you're in charge of today won't affect the fate of the nations.

You can relax.

The rooms aren't in quite as big a rush to be painted. The day can end without your having to read the newspaper. You can be thankful your old car is at least good transportation.

You can wait.

The hours you spend listening to the goofballs on radio call-in shows will seem a waste. The urgency of telling people about Jesus will burn in your spirit. The people you haven't told lately how much you love them will be the next phone call you make or the next letter you write.

You can act.

You'll want to be holy, to be pure, to be real.

You can live. Oh boy, how you can live!

> "Our inheritance is as sure as morning. Why are we so reluctant to leave this dingy world? Things really are better further on."
>
> —Calvin Miller

NEXT UP *Love the Lord your God with all your heart, all your soul, and all your mind—and your neighbor as yourself. That'll keep you on the right track from start to finish.*